AQA Religious Studies B

Worship and Key Beliefs

GCSE

Marianne Fleming
Anne Jordan
Peter Smith
David Worden

Series editor
Cynthia Bartlett

Nelson Thornes

Text © Marianne Fleming, Anne Jordan, Peter Smith and David Worden 2009
Original illustrations © Nelson Thornes Ltd 2009

The right of Marianne Fleming, Anne Jordan, Peter Smith and David Worden to be identified as authors of this work has been asserted by them in accordance with the Copyright, Designs and Patents Act 1988.

All rights reserved. No part of this publication may be reproduced or transmitted in any form or by any means, electronic or mechanical, including photocopy, recording or any information storage and retrieval system, without permission in writing from the publisher or under licence from the Copyright Licensing Agency Limited, of Saffron House, 6-10 Kirby Street, London EC1N 8TS.

Any person who commits any unauthorised act in relation to this publication may be liable to criminal prosecution and civil claims for damages.

Published in 2009 by:
Nelson Thornes Ltd
Delta Place
27 Bath Road
CHELTENHAM
GL53 7TH
United Kingdom

09 10 11 12 13 / 10 9 8 7 6 5 4 3 2 1

A catalogue record for this book is available from the British Library

978-1-4085-0517-5

Cover photograph: Courtesy of Rex Features/Design Pics Inc

Illustrations by Paul McCaffrey (c/o Sylvie Poggio Artists Agency), Jane Taylor, Steve Ballinger and Hart McLeod

Page make-up by Hart McLeod, Cambridge

Printed in Spain by GraphyCems

Photo Acknowledgements

Alamy 1.6A; **Alamy/Dave Stamboulis** 4.4A; **Alamy/Eddie Gerald** 1.6D; **Alamy/Guy Harrop** 5.8B; **Alamy/Ian Goodrick** 1.2B; **Alamy/Nir Alon** 3.3B; **Alamy/Shangara Singh** 1.11Avi; **Circa Religion Photo Library/Bipin Mistry** 1.5B; **Corbis/Stringer/India/Reuters** 3.10A; **Fotalia** 1.1D, 1.3B, 1.5C, 1.6B, 1.6C, 1.7B, 1.7C, 1.8B, 1.10A, 1.10B, 2.1A, 2.3A, 2.3B, 2.4A, 2.4B, 2.5A, 2.5B, 2.7A, 2.7B, 2.8A, 2.8B, 2.9A, 2.9B, 2.9C, 2.10A, 2 (assessment), 3.1A, 3.1B, 3.6A, 3.6B, 3.7A, 3.8A, 4.5A, 4.6A, 4.8B, 4.10A, 5.1A, 5.4A, 5.4B, 5.5A, 5.7A, 5.7B, 5.7C, 5.9A, 5.10A, 6.3A, 6.5A, 6.7A, 6.8A, 6.8B, 6.9A, 6.10B, 6 (assessment); **Getty** 3.4A, 4.7B, 4.9B, 5.7D, 6.5C; **Istock** 1.1A, 1.1B, 1.1C, 1.2A, 1.3A, 1.3C, 1.7A, 1.8C, 1.11Ai, 1.11Aii, 1.11Aiii, 1.11Aiv, 1.11Av, 2.1B, 2.2A, 2.2B, 2.6A, 2.6C, 2.10B, 3.2A, 3.2B, 3.4C, 3.5A, 3.9B, 4.1A, 4.2A, 4.2B, 4.3A, 4.6B, 4.6C, 4.7A, 4.8A, 5.1B, 5.2A, 5.3A, 5.3B, 5.6A, 5.6B, 5.8A, 5.9B, 5.10B, 5 (assessment A), 5 (assessment B), 6.1A, 6.1B, 6.2A, 6.2B, 6.5A, 6.6B; **Kapila Thilakarathne** 1.3D; **Peter Smith** 6.3B, 6.4B, 6.6A, 6.9B, 6.9C, 6.10A; **Rex Features** 6.1C, 6.4A; **Sacred Destinations Photography/Holly Hayes** 1.9A; **World Religions Photo Library/P. Gapper** 4.9A.

Text Acknowledgements

Scripture quotations taken from the Holy Bible, New International Version. Copyright © 1978, 1984 by International Bible Society. Used by permission of Hodder & Stoughton, a division of Hodder Headline Ltd. All rights reserved. "NIV" is a registered trademark of International Bible Society. UK trademark number 1448790.

1.2 Barrett, Simon. 'New $40 Million Hindu Temple Opens, While Millions Starve!' Extract from http://www.bloggernews.net/18822, 22nd July 2007. Reprinted with kind permission of the author. 2.7, 5.2, 5.4, 5.5 Extracts from 'The Holy Quran Translation And Commentary' by Abdullah Yusuf Ali. Reprinted with permission of IPCI - Islamic Vision, 434 Coventry Road, Small Heath, Birmingham B10 0UG UK. 3.9 Short quotes from the 'Hajj' Documentary on Channel 4, found at http://www.channel4.com/culture/microsites/H/hajj/index.html. © Channel 4. Reprinted with kind permission. 4.5 The English Translation of the Apostle's Creed by the International Consultation on English Texts ICET. 5.7 Short extract from the Christian Marriage Service. Reprinted with permission of Church House Publishing. 6.1 Definition of 'Authority' from Concise Oxford Dictionary. Reprinted with permission of Oxford University Press.

Contents

Introduction ... 5

1 Places of worship ... 8
1.1 Introduction ... 8
1.2 The money spent on religious buildings ... 10
1.3 Places of worship in Buddhism ... 12
1.4 Places of worship in Christianity ... 14
1.5 Places of worship in Hinduism ... 16
1.6 Places of worship in Islam ... 18
1.7 Places of worship in Judaism ... 20
1.8 Places of worship in Sikhism ... 22
1.9 The value of religious buildings ... 24
1.10 Places of worship in the community ... 26
Chapter 1: Assessment guidance ... 28

2 Worship ... 30
2.1 Worship ... 30
2.2 Days of worship ... 32
2.3 Aids to worship and prayer ... 34
2.4 Prayer aids ... 36
2.5 Buddhist worship ... 38
2.6 Christian worship ... 40
2.7 Hindu worship ... 42
2.8 Muslim worship ... 44
2.9 Jewish worship ... 46
2.10 Sikh worship ... 48
Chapter 2: Assessment guidance ... 50

3 Pilgrimage ... 52
3.1 What is a pilgrimage? ... 52
3.2 Buddhist holy places ... 54
3.3 Christian holy places (1) ... 56
3.4 Christian holy places (2) ... 58
3.5 Hindu holy places ... 60
3.6 Muslim holy places ... 62
3.7 Jewish holy places ... 64
3.8 Sikh holy places ... 66
3.9 How pilgrimage can change a life ... 68
3.10 The importance of pilgrimage to a religion ... 70
Chapter 3: Assessment guidance ... 72

4 Origins and beliefs ... 74
4.1 Beginnings: Hinduism, Buddhism and Sikhism ... 74
4.2 Beginnings: Judaism, Christianity and Islam ... 76
4.3 Beliefs about God ... 78
4.4 Buddhist beliefs ... 80
4.5 Christian beliefs ... 82
4.6 Hindu beliefs ... 84
4.7 Muslim beliefs ... 86
4.8 Jewish beliefs ... 88
4.9 Sikh beliefs ... 90
4.10 The soul and the afterlife ... 92
Chapter 4 : Assessment guidance ... 94

5 Practices and belonging — 96

- 5.1 Introduction: Buddhist and Christian behaviour codes and duties — 96
- 5.2 Hindu and Muslim behaviour codes and duties — 98
- 5.3 Jewish and Sikh behaviour codes and duties — 100
- 5.4 Dietary laws — 102
- 5.5 Prayer and meditation — 104
- 5.6 Rites of passage: birth and initiation ceremonies — 106
- 5.7 Rites of passage: marriages and funerals — 108
- 5.8 Key festivals: Buddhism and Christianity — 110
- 5.9 Key festivals: Hinduism and Islam — 112
- 5.10 Key festivals: Judaism and Sikhism — 114

Chapter 5: Assessment guidance — 116

6 Religious authority — 118

- 6.1 Introduction: authority and leadership — 118
- 6.2 Leadership of religion — 120
- 6.3 Holy books and leadership — 122
- 6.4 Authority in Buddhism — 124
- 6.5 Authority in Christianity — 126
- 6.6 Authority in Hinduism — 128
- 6.7 Authority in Islam — 130
- 6.8 Authority in Judaism — 132
- 6.9 Authority in Sikhism — 134
- 6.10 Evaluation of leadership — 136

Chapter 6: Assessment guidance — 138

Glossary — 140

Index — 143

Nelson Thornes and AQA

Nelson Thornes has worked in partnership with AQA to make sure that this book offers you the best possible support for your GCSE course. All the content has been approved by the senior examining team at AQA, so you can be sure that it gives you just what you need when you are preparing for your exams.

■ How to use this book

This book covers everything you need for your course.

Learning Objectives

At the beginning of each section or topic you'll find a list of Learning Objectives based on the requirements of the specification, so you can make sure you are covering everything you need to know for the exam.

Objectives
Objectives
Objectives
Objectives
First objective.
Second objective.

AQA Examiner's Tips

Don't forget to look at the AQA Examiner's Tips throughout the book to help you with your study and prepare for your exam.

AQA Examiner's tip

Don't forget to look at the AQA Examiner's Tips throughout the book to help you with your study and prepare for your exam.

AQA Examination-style Questions

These offer opportunities to practise doing questions in the style that you can expect in your exam so that you can be fully prepared on the day.

AQA examination questions are reproduced by permission of the Assessment and Qualifications Alliance.

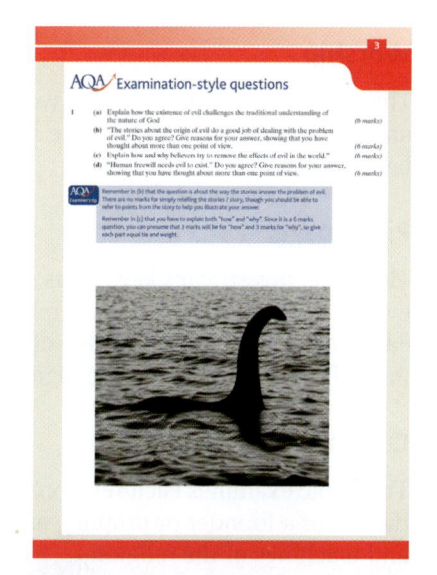

Visit **www.nelsonthornes.com/aqagcse** for more information.

AQA GCSE Worship and Key Beliefs

This book is written specifically for GCSE students studying the AQA Religious Studies Specification B *Unit 6 Worship and Key Beliefs*. The course enables students to explore the key beliefs, teachings and practices of at least **two** of the six major world faiths (Buddhism, Christianity, Hinduism, Islam, Judaism, Sikhism) and allows for comparison and contrast of different aspects of two of them.

The unit will help you develop your knowledge, skills and understanding of religion by investigating places of worship, practices and functions of worship, pilgrimage, origins and key beliefs, religious practices, and sources of authority. You will reflect on the impact and importance of these aspects for believers so that you can explain your own reasoned opinions.

◼ Topics in this unit

In the examination you will be asked to answer four questions, based on four of the following six topics:

Places of worship

This topic examines religious buildings, the symbolism of their exterior and interior features and furnishings, their use and role in the community, and their value to believers and to the religion.

Worship

This topic explores how people worship in public and at home, and its importance and value to believers.

Pilgrimage

This topic investigates key places of pilgrimage, the events, people, practices and symbolism linked to each, and the impact and value of pilgrimage on individual believers and the religion itself.

Origins and beliefs

This topic examines each religion's origins, including the life of a founder or prophet, and the main beliefs and teachings of the religion.

Practices and belonging

This topic explores the importance and value for believers of religious practices including behaviour codes, duties, dietary laws, prayer and meditation, rites of passage and key festivals.

Religious authority

This topic examines the role, importance and value of different sources of authority for believers. These include people (founders, prophets and religious leaders), tradition, community, holy books and the relative merits of these as sources of authority.

◼ Assessment guidance

The questions set in the examination will allow you to refer in your answers to the religion(s) you have studied. To encourage you to practise examination-type questions, each chapter has an assessment guidance section at the end. Each question in the examination will include a three-mark and a six-mark evaluation question. This section will help you to write better answers yourself, if you understand what the examiners are looking for when they mark these questions. To assist you in this, you will be asked to mark a sample answer for yourself – using the mark scheme below. Make sure that you understand the differences between the standard of answer for each level, and what you need to do to achieve full marks.

Examination questions will test two assessment objectives:

| AO1 | Describe, explain and analyse, using knowledge and understanding. | 50% |
| AO2 | Use evidence and reasoned argument to express and evaluate personal responses, informed insights, and differing viewpoints. | 50% |

Levels of response mark scheme for six-mark evaluation questions

Levels	Criteria for AO1	Criteria for AO2	Quality of written communication	Marks
0	Nothing relevant or worthy of credit	An unsupported opinion or no relevant evaluation	The candidate's presentation, spelling, punctuation and grammar seriously obstruct understanding	0 marks
Level 1	Something relevant or worthy of credit	An opinion supported by simple reason	The candidate presents some relevant information in a simple form. The text produced is usually legible. Spelling, punctuation and grammar allow meaning to be derived, although errors are sometimes obstructive	1 mark
Level 2	Elementary knowledge and understanding, e.g. two simple points	An opinion supported by one developed or two simple reasons		2 marks
Level 3	Sound knowledge and understanding	An opinion supported by one well developed reason or several simple reasons. **N.B. Candidates who make no religious comment should not achieve more than Level 3**	The candidate presents relevant information in a way which assists with the communication of meaning. The text produced is legible. Spelling, punctuation and grammar are sufficiently accurate not to obscure meaning	3 marks
Level 4	A clear knowledge and understanding with some development	An opinion supported by two developed reasons with reference to religion		4 marks
Level 5	A detailed answer with some analysis, as appropriate	Evidence of reasoned consideration of two different points of view, showing informed insights and knowledge and understanding of religion	The candidate presents relevant information coherently, employing structure and style to render meaning clear. The text produced is legible. Spelling, punctuation and grammar are sufficiently accurate to render meaning clear	5 marks
Level 6	A full and coherent answer showing good analysis, as appropriate	A well-argued response, with evidence of reasoned consideration of two different points of view showing informed insights and ability to apply knowledge and understanding of religion effectively		6 marks

Note: In evaluation answers to questions worth only 3 marks, the first three levels apply. Questions which are marked out of 3 marks do not ask for two views, but simply for your opinion.

Successful study of this unit will result in a Short Course GCSE award. Study of one further unit will provide a Full Course GCSE award. Other units in Specification B which may be taken to achieve a Full Course GCSE award are:

- Unit 1 Religion and Citizenship
- Unit 2 Religion and Life Issues
- Unit 3 Religion and Morality
- Unit 4 Religious Philosophy and Ultimate Questions
- Unit 5 Religious Expression in Society.

1 Places of worship

1.1 Introduction

What is meant by a place of worship?

A **place of worship** is a place where specific acts of religious praise, honour or devotion take place. These acts of worship are usually directed to a supernatural being such as God, but occasionally they may make special reference or show devotion to a person considered to be important to the religion. Buddhists do not worship God, but during acts of worship pray and meditate to gain spiritual knowledge and understanding.

Research activity

Using the internet or a library, find out why the Nabawi mosque is an important place of worship in Islam.

A place of worship may be a building, a **shrine** or a special place. Different religions have different names for their places of worship, and their designs will also vary. Some places of worship are very grand and ornate, whereas others are simple.

In this book, you are going to examine six of the world's major religions – Buddhism, Christianity, Hinduism, Islam, Judaism and Sikhism. The names used for the places of worship in these religions are:

- **Buddhism:** temple or stupa
- **Christianity:** chapel, church or cathedral
- **Hinduism:** temple or mandir
- **Islam:** mosque
- **Judaism:** synagogue
- **Sikhism:** temple or gurdwara.

Sometimes the place of worship is in the home of the religious believer. For example, Hindus will offer prayers at a shrine in their homes. Muslims will perform the five daily prayers in their homes. Muslims are allowed to pray anywhere so long as the place is clean and they use a prayer mat. Even if Muslims are not worshipping in a mosque, the place where the Muslim puts the prayer mat becomes a temporary mosque.

Objectives

Examine what is meant by a place of worship.

Investigate why there are places of worship.

Key terms

Place of worship: a building or other location where an individual or a group of people comes to perform acts of religious worship.

Shrine: a place of worship considered holy because of its link with some sacred person or thing.

links

See page 24 for a definition of the term 'spiritual', or you can look it up in the Glossary at the back of this book.

A *The Nabawi mosque is the second holiest mosque in Islam*

Chapter 1 Places of worship 9

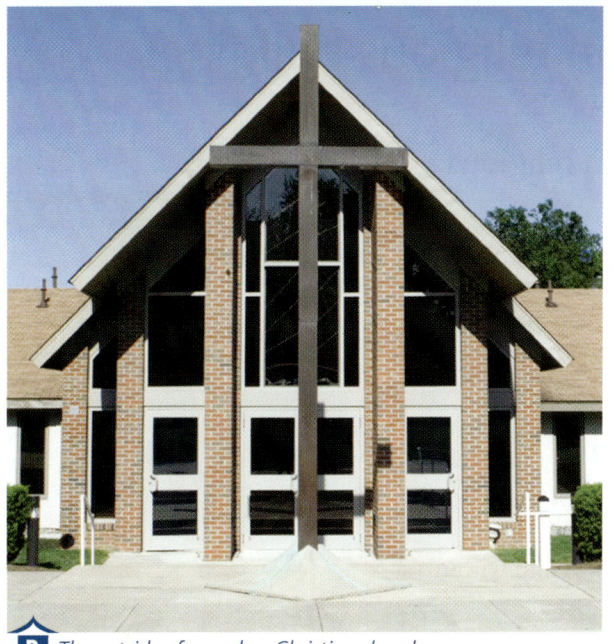

B *The outside of a modern Christian church*

C *The Golden Temple of Amritsar is the holiest place for Sikhs*

Why are there places of worship?

There are many reasons why religions have places of worship:

- The design of the inside of the place of worship can support the kind of worship that believers want to perform.
- They provide a place where the community of believers can come together for worship.
- They provide a place where the atmosphere is right for prayer and meditation.
- It is more appropriate to have a special place in which to worship God or to seek enlightenment.
- The building of a beautiful place of worship in itself can be an act of worship to God.

Discussion activity

With a partner, in a small group or as a whole class, discuss the following statement: 'It is better to worship God on your own rather than in a place where there are other worshippers.' Do you agree? Give reasons for your answer, showing that you have thought about more than one point of view.

AQA Examiner's tip

Make sure that you are able to name the places of worship for the religions you have studied.

D *A Buddhist temple*

Activities

1. Explain what is meant by a 'shrine'.
2. Explain why people have places of worship.
3. 'People only need a place of worship in their homes.' Do you agree? Give reasons for your answer, showing that you have thought about more than one point of view.

Summary

You should now be able to explain what is meant by a place of worship and why there are places of worship.

1.2 The money spent on religious buildings

■ The argument about spending money on religious buildings

Most people would agree that places of worship are part of everybody's heritage and should be maintained, and many often get involved with fundraising for repairs to places of worship. English Heritage and the Heritage Lottery Fund agreed a budget of £25m for 2008–9 to support repair work on listed places of worship in England.

Reasons for spending money on places of worship

- The beauty of a place of worship shows the importance of the religion to the people.
- The building needs to be designed to suit the way of worship within the religion.
- Buildings such as the Swaminarayan temple are built by donation and, for the believers, this is an act of worship in itself.
- A beautiful place of worship shows adoration of God.
- If places of worship are not maintained, then it would appear that people do not care about their religion.

Reasons for not spending money on places of worship

- Prayer and meditation do not require an ornate place of worship.
- If the building is too large and ornate, it could distract people from the act of worship.
- An important part of worship is helping the less fortunate and this is where the money should go, not on expensive places of worship.
- People can worship in their homes so they do not need to build places of worship.
- God would not want a place of worship to be showy.

> **Objectives**
> Consider the money spent on religious buildings.

Case study

The new Swaminarayan Mandir temple in Toronto, Canada

A new Hindu temple was opened in Toronto, Canada in July 2007. The temple cost $40m (about £21m) and was funded by donations from Hindus all over the world. The work involved more than 2000 Indian craftsmen and about 400 volunteers from Toronto's Hindu community. The construction of the stone building includes 24 000 hand-carved pieces of Turkish limestone and Italian Carrara marble, which were shipped across the ocean and assembled in Toronto. The marble floor is electrically heated to make worshipping in winter a bearable experience for the barefoot devotees. The temple can hold up to 2000 people at one time.

A *The Swaminarayan Mandir, Toronto, Canada*

Discussion activity

Read the following view of Simon Barrett about the building of the new Swaminarayan Mandir temple. What do you think? Explain your opinion.

> *My [job] is working with the homeless, and working poor, people with no place to live, no food, and rapidly declining self-esteem, and health. Life on the streets is hard, survive 5 years, you age 20. I look at that $40 million and just wonder how much 'low cost' housing it could become? I look at the fact that much of the work was done in India and shipped to Canada, OK, Canadians may not be great stone workers, but we sure know how to build structures that can withstand the environment.*
>
> *The Swaminarayan Mandir temple may be a wonderful piece of work; it may even be a classic. But give me $40 million and I could do something useful. Something that is renewable and sustainable, something that could actually help people.*
>
> Simon Barrett, 22 July 2007

Activities

1. a. Read the teachings of Muhammad and Jesus in the Beliefs and teachings boxes. Write an explanation of these teachings in your own words.
   b. How do you think people might apply these teachings to the building of places of worship?

2. 'God would prefer people to feed the hungry people of the world rather than spend money on building beautiful places of worship.' What do you think? Explain your opinion.

Extension activity

1. a. Using the internet or a library, find out about the building of a new place of worship somewhere in the world.
   b. Write a newspaper report about the construction of the building, including reference to the cost, design and building materials.

Summary

You should now be able to discuss the arguments for and against spending money on places of worship.

Beliefs and teachings

The prophet Muhammad teaches that Muslims can pray anywhere

The earth has been made for me (and for my followers) as a 'masjid' [a place of worship] and a means of purification. Therefore, any one of my followers can pray whenever the time of a prayer is due.

Hadith

B *The new Sikh gurdwara at Gravesend, Kent*

Beliefs and teachings

Jesus teaches people to pray in secret

And when you pray, do not be like the hypocrites, for they love to pray standing in the synagogues and on the street corners to be seen by men. I tell you the truth, they have received their reward in full. But when you pray, go into your room, close the door and pray to your Father, who is unseen. Then your Father, who sees what is done in secret, will reward you.

Matthew 6:5–6

AQA Examiner's tip

Make sure that you know the different reasons religious believers have for and against spending money on places of worship.

1.3 Places of worship in Buddhism

Buddhist places of worship

Buddhists worship in **temples** or at shrines or **stupas**, where they will show respect to the Buddha or other leading teachers. Buddhists do not worship a god but work towards enlightenment; that is the understanding of the meaning of life.

Buddhist places of worship are designed to create an atmosphere of calm and peace, to aid reflection and meditation. Buddhist temples will always have a statue of the Buddha that is placed higher than the worshippers to show the honour due to him, and an altar at which offerings may be made.

> **Objectives**
>
> Describe the exterior and interior features of Buddhist places of worship.
>
> Explain the symbolism of the exterior and interior of Buddhist places of worship.

A A typical statue of the Buddha

B A Buddhist temple in Bangkok

The exterior of Buddhist stupas and temples

There are often stalls near to the place of worship selling flowers, food or incense because offerings are made by individuals as part of their worship.

Stupas are buildings that contain relics of the Buddha himself or of another great Buddhist leader, or a scripture. They will have a shrine in front of them at which people sit and meditate or make offerings. In some smaller temples or at a shrine in the home, there may be a miniature stupa. In a home, it may be a model of a stupa or one containing family relics.

The **symbolism** of stupas and temples is important. The shape of the stupa or temple is said to represent the five elements (fire, air, earth, water and wisdom). The square base or foundation represents the earth, with the dome as water. The stone fence around the base

> **Key terms**
>
> **Temple:** a building used for religious or spiritual activities.
>
> **Stupa:** a burial mound.
>
> **Symbolism:** when an image or action stands for something else.

represents fire, and the pyramid shape above links to air. The pinnacle on the top is symbolic of the enlightenment and wisdom that Buddhists are seeking.

Extension activity

1. a Using the internet or a library, find out more about the symbolism of the stupa.
   b Draw a stupa and label the symbolism of each section.

The interior of Buddhist places of worship

The most important part of a Buddhist temple is the shrine hall containing the statue or picture of the Buddha, before which the worshippers make their offerings. Beside the image of the Buddha, there will be a vase or tray of flowers. The flowers symbolise that living things die. The number of flowers has meaning: for example, one flower teaches the unity of all things. The enlightenment the worshippers are seeking is represented by a lighted candle or lamp. Incense is burnt and, as the fragrance fills the room, worshippers are reminded that Buddhist teaching has spread throughout the world. There will often be Buddhist texts on the walls or painted rolls, called thangkhas, as a reminder of aspects of the faith's teaching.

C *The Golden Stupa in Bangkok*

Discussion activity

With a partner, in a small group or as a whole class, discuss the following statement: 'The use of symbols does not help Buddhists to worship.' Do you agree? Give reasons for your answer, showing that you have thought about more than one point of view.

D *The shrine room at Letchworth Buddhist Temple*

Activities

1. Explain what you would find in the shrine hall of a Buddhist place of worship and explain the symbolism of the features you have chosen.

2. 'As Buddhists do not worship God, they do not need places of worship.' Do you agree? Give reasons for your answer, showing that you have thought about more than one point of view.

AQA Examiner's tip

Make sure that you can explain both the external and internal features of a Buddhist place of worship.

Remember, Buddhists also worship at shrines in their own homes.

∞links

See pages 38–39 to find out more about Buddhist worship.

Summary

You should now be able to describe and explain the symbolism of the exterior and interior features of Buddhist places of worship.

1.4 Places of worship in Christianity

■ Christian worship

The different forms of worship within Christian denominations shape the design of the place of worship. Christian places of worship include **churches**, chapels and **cathedrals**.

Worship in the home

Christians worship in their homes using prayer aids that include the Bible, prayer books, statues, **icons** and crosses or crucifixes. To help concentration, Catholics use a set of beads called a Rosary.

The House Church is a group of Christians who meet for worship in homes. They believe that their informal style of worship is how Jesus intended his followers to worship God.

> **Research activity**
>
> 1. **a** Using the internet or a library, find out about **one** of the following Christian places of worship:
>   - Baptist church
>   - Friends' meeting house
>   - Salvation Army citadel
>   **b** Write a description of the internal and external features of the place of worship you have chosen.
>   **c** Explain the symbolism of the main features.

■ The exterior of Christian places of worship

Some churches have spires, which represent a symbolic 'finger' pointing the way to heaven as a reminder that it is through Christian worship that the way is opened to God. There may be a bell tower from which the bells are rung to call worshippers to prayer.

Orthodox churches have a circular dome that represents heaven and the eternity of God, and reminds people that God's blessing is gained by accepting salvation through Christ. Many Christian churches are built in the shape of a cross because Christians believe that Jesus died on the cross to save them from sin. The windows are often stained glass, featuring stories from the Bible or the lives of leading Christians.

> **Objectives**
>
> Describe the exterior and interior features of Christian places of worship.
>
> Explain the symbolism of the exterior and interior of Christian places of worship.

> **Key terms**
>
> **Church:** a building in which Christians worship.
>
> **Cathedral:** the principal/main church of a bishop's diocese.
>
> **Icon:** painting or mosaic of Jesus or the saints. Icons are more than simply aids to prayer, as they are seen as being filled with the spirit of the person shown.

∞ links

See the Glossary at the back of this book for a definition of the term 'symbolism'.

A Some churches have a spire

The interior of Christian places of worship

The interior of Roman Catholic and Anglican (Church of England) churches

The central feature in the Roman Catholic and Anglican churches is the holiest part of the church – the **altar**. It is the focal point of the most important service in these two denominations, Holy Communion. Candles are lit on the altar at the beginning of each service as a reminder that Christ, the Light of the World, will be present during the service.

Below the altar are the **pulpit** and the lectern, a stand on which the Bible rests and from which Bible readings are given. The **font** is usually situated near the door to symbolise that it is through baptism that people gain entry into the Christian faith. Catholic churches also have **confessionals**.

The interior of Orthodox churches

Inside an Orthodox church, the altar is hidden behind a screen (the iconostasis) painted with pictures of Christ, the Virgin Mary and saints. The screen is a reminder of the separation between heaven and earth. In the centre of the screen are the Royal Doors, which are opened and closed during the service of Holy Communion to represent the link between heaven and earth brought through Jesus' death.

The interior of Methodist, Baptist and United Reformed churches

The focal point in Methodist, Baptist and United Reformed churches is the pulpit because these denominations believe that salvation comes through the Word of God. Therefore, the most important part of worship is listening to Bible readings or to sermons explaining God's Word. There will be a communion table instead of an altar, because they believe that the service of Holy Communion is a memorial to strengthen faith and fellowship.

Some Methodist and United Reformed churches will have a font at the front of the church and others may have a bowl to act as a font.

Activity

1. a Look at the photograph of an Anglican church. Name the main features found in the church that you can see in the photograph.
   b Explain what each feature is used for in an Anglican church.

Summary

You should now be able to describe and explain the symbolism of the exterior and interior features of Christian places of worship.

Key terms

Altar: a symbol of the table used by Jesus at the Last Supper – it is a type of table used for Holy Communion.

Pulpit: raised area from which the sermon is preached.

Font: receptacle for the holy water of baptism.

Confessional: a place where a priest hears a person confess their sins (in a Roman Catholic church).

links

See page 41 to find out what is meant by Holy Communion.

AQA Examiner's tip

Remember that the places of worship belonging to the different denominations in Christianity often have different internal features from each other.

B *The interior of an Anglican church*

links

See pages 40–41 to find out more about Christian worship.

1.5 Places of worship in Hinduism

■ Hindu worship

Hindus believe in one Supreme Being, Brahman, from whom everything in the universe comes. Brahman is formless and beyond human understanding, but takes many forms in order to be known in the world. Hindus believe that there are many gods and goddesses that represent different attributes of Brahman, and they will be represented in the places of worship, by statues and/or pictures. The leading gods and goddesses can be recognised by symbols associated with them.

Hindus worship in temples called **mandirs**, dedicated to, and regarded as the home of, a particular god or goddess. The building is designed to represent the order of the universe and the harmonious relationship between humans and the earth. The temple is not only a place of worship, but an object of worship in itself. Every part of the temple is holy and treated with respect, and will have the sacred symbol Om representing Brahman, the source of all existence. This helps Hindus to concentrate on Brahman. Hindus perform **puja** (daily worship) either at a mandir, or at shrines within the home.

> **Objectives**
>
> Describe the exterior and interior features of Hindu places of worship.
>
> Explain the symbolism of the exterior and interior of Hindu places of worship.

> **Key terms**
>
> **Mandir:** a Hindu temple.
> **Puja:** Hindu worship in the home or temple.
> **Murti (Moorti):** image or deity used as a focus of worship and offerings.

> **Research activity**
>
> Using the internet or a library, research the symbols associated with the gods:
> - Brahma
> - Vishnu
> - Shiva.

A *A Hindu boy praying before the shrine in his home*

B *The Hindu symbol for Om*

Worship in the home

Puja in the home is performed either in a separate room or at a shrine. There will be a statue or picture of the god or goddess to whom the family directs their prayers. There will be a lamp close to the shrine that is lit during worship to represent the light of knowledge.

∞ links

See page 42 to find out more about the symbol Om.

The exterior of Hindu places of worship

In purpose-built Hindu temples, there will be a gateway entrance and a tall tower that stands over the **murti** of the god or goddess. The temple will stand within a walled enclosure and be built so that it faces the rising sun.

There will be a large stone statue of the creature that is said to be the vehicle of the god or goddess. For example, the god Shiva rides Nandi the bull, which represents the power and energy of Shiva. The vehicle symbolises the various forces the god controls in the universe. These energies are also found in humans, and the vehicle is a reminder that these energies need to be controlled.

Extension activity

Using the internet or a library, find out more about the symbolism of vehicles that the Hindu gods and goddesses ride.

At the entrance to the temple, there is a bell that people ring as they enter to show their presence to the god or goddess to whom the mandir is dedicated. The worshippers remove their shoes and wash their hands to avoid bringing any dirt into the holy place, and to symbolise the purity of the place.

C *The exterior of a Hindu temple dedicated to the elephant god, Ganesha*

The interior of Hindu places of worship

Inside there will be murtis of various gods and goddesses. The principal god of the temple is usually in a shrine with a canopy over it, which is the focus of worship. The image of the god will be dressed in rich clothing that is changed regularly by the priest. Offerings of food, money, incense and flowers are made at the shrine as a symbolic way of saying thank you to the gods for all the things that they have provided.

There will be no seats and worshippers sit on the floor to show their devotion to the gods.

Discussion activity

In pairs, discuss why you think that the murtis are dressed in rich clothing and the clothing is changed regularly. Give reasons for your answer.

Summary

You should now be able to describe and explain the symbolism of the exterior and interior features of Hindu places of worship.

Activities

1. Write a description of the exterior of a Hindu mandir.
2. Write a description of the interior of a Hindu mandir.

∞ links

See pages 42–43 to find out more about Hindu worship.

AQA Examiner's tip

Remember that many Hindus perform daily puja in their homes, so make sure you can describe a shrine in a Hindu home.

1.6 Places of worship in Islam

Worship in Islam

Muslims believe in one God (Allah). To keep Allah in their thoughts at all times, Muslims pray a minimum of five times a day. All that is required for a place of worship is that it is a clean and appropriate place, as the whole world is believed to be a **mosque**.

Worship in the home

When praying at home, Muslims usually put down a prayer mat to ensure the place of prayer is clean and to show proper respect to Allah. Some Muslims use a string of 33 or 99 prayer beads as an aid to prayer. These beads represent the 99 beautiful names of Allah. The Muslim moves the beads along and recites the names of Allah as they pray.

A *Muslims use a prayer mat when not praying at the mosque*

B *The exterior of a mosque*

C *The courtyard of a purpose-built mosque*

The exterior of Muslim places of worship

Purpose-built mosques are usually built in the form of a square, with an open courtyard in the centre and running water for Muslims to wash in preparation for prayer.

The mosque will have a tall tower called a **minaret**, which is where the call to prayer (the Adhan) is given five times a day, and a dome as a reminder of the universe and the great love of Allah. The dome is often green as a reminder of the beauty of Allah's creation.

At the entrance to the mosque, there are shoe racks on which the worshippers put their shoes before entering the prayer hall.

Objectives

Describe the exterior and interior features of Muslim places of worship.

Explain the symbolism of the exterior and interior of Muslim places of worship.

Key terms

Mosque: the Muslim place of worship.

Minaret: in Islam, the tower of the mosque from which the muezzin calls the faithful to pray.

Research activity

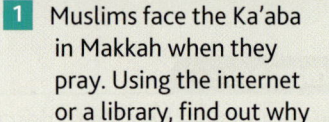

1. Muslims face the Ka'aba in Makkah when they pray. Using the internet or a library, find out why Muslims face this direction for prayer.

Discussion activity

With a partner, in a small group or as a whole class, discuss the following statement: 'It does not matter the direction in which you pray so long as you pray.' Do you agree? Give reasons for your answer, showing that you have thought about more than one point of view.

The interior of Muslim places of worship

The prayer hall is a large open space without seats, with a separate area or prayer hall for women to pray.

The worshippers stand in lines facing the direction of the Ka'aba in Makkah. The direction is known as the **qiblah** and it is indicated by an alcove in the wall called the **mihrab**. Near to the mihrab is the **minbar**, a short flight of stairs with a platform on top to form a pulpit from which the imam (leader of the service) gives a sermon during the Friday midday prayers.

On the walls there are usually quotations from the Qur'an, the holy book of Islam, but no images or pictures of Allah, who is beyond human understanding. Nor will there be images or pictures of Prophet Muhammad or any other holy figure, as it is felt that this could give the impression that it is the image that is being worshipped. Because Islam has forbidden the use of images, intricate patterns are used as decoration instead.

D *The alcove called the mihrab, indicating the direction of Makkah*

Research activity

2. Calligraphy, which means beautiful writing, is used in Islam for the Qur'anic quotations that decorate the walls of the mosque. Using the internet or a library, find out more about the use of calligraphy in Islam.

Activity

'Muslims are able to pray anywhere they like, so it is not necessary to build mosques.' Do you agree? Give reasons for your answer, showing that you have thought about more than one point of view.

Summary

You should now be able to describe and explain the symbolism of the exterior and interior features of Muslim places of worship.

links

Look back to page 15 to remind yourself of what is meant by a pulpit or sermon.

Key terms

Qiblah: the direction Muslims face when praying, towards Makkah.

Mihrab: niche or alcove in the mosque wall to show the direction of Makkah.

Minbar: a platform on which the Imam stands to deliver the Khutbah to let the congregation see him.

links

See pages 44–45 to find out more about Muslim worship.

AQA Examiner's tip

Make sure that you understand the meaning of the different terms used for parts of the mosque.

1.7 Places of worship in Judaism

Worship in Judaism

Jews worship one God, with whom they believe that they have a special relationship. Their lifestyle is guided by their belief in God, and these beliefs have an influence on their worship at home and in the synagogue. Often, objects are used to help Jews focus their attention in worship, such as special items of clothing.

Worship in the home

Jewish men pray three times a day and this will often take place in the home. Home worship also involves obeying the laws found in the Torah, and this includes the dietary laws.

The most important worship that takes place in the Jewish home occurs each Sabbath. Attached to the doorpost of a Jewish home is a small decorated box called a mezuzah, which contains the Jewish statement of faith, the Shema.

The exterior of Jewish places of worship

There are no rules stating what a synagogue should look like on the outside, but there are usually symbols associated with Judaism that make it recognisable. There may be a menorah (seven-branched candelabra) and/or the six-pointed Star of David, a great Jewish king. Stained glass is often used in the windows of synagogues and these may relate to events from Jewish history.

A *The exterior of a synagogue*

The interior of Jewish places of worship

The most important feature inside the rectangular prayer hall of the synagogue is the Ark where the Torah is kept. The Torah is handwritten on parchment scrolls. The Ark is a cupboard with either doors or curtains that are only opened to take out the relevant scroll during worship. The Ark is named after the Ark of the Covenant that held the Ten Commandments in Moses' time, and is set in the wall facing Jerusalem where the Temple, destroyed in 70 CE, stood. These scrolls are believed to contain the Word of God and are treated with the greatest respect.

> **Objectives**
>
> Describe the exterior and interior features of Jewish places of worship.
>
> Explain the symbolism of the exterior and interior of Jewish places of worship.

> **Key terms**
>
> **Synagogue:** a building for Jewish public prayer, study and gathering.
>
> **Torah:** the five books of Moses and first section of the Tenakh – the law; the whole of Jewish teaching.
>
> **Menorah:** candle-holder with seven branches. It is often placed prominently in the synagogue as a reminder of the Jewish Temple.

> **Activities**
>
> 1. Explain how you might be able to identify a building as a synagogue from the outside.
>
> 2. Describe and explain the main features of the prayer hall in a synagogue.

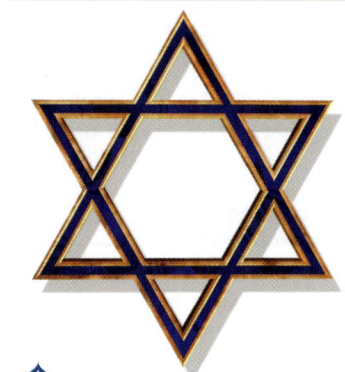

B *The Star of David is called the Magan David*

Chapter 1 Places of worship **21**

C *The focal point in the prayer hall is the Ark and the bimah*

The **ner tamid** (eternal light) is kept burning at all times in front of the Ark as a reminder that God is eternal. Above the Ark, there are usually two tablets on which the first two words of each of the Ten Commandments are written in Hebrew. Nearby will be the menorah, which was always kept alight in the Temple.

In the centre of the synagogue, there will be the **bimah**, a raised platform from which the rabbi (Jewish religious leader) leads the service and from which the Torah is read. There is seating on three sides facing the bimah. In Orthodox synagogues, the women are seated separately from the men, often in a gallery, but in Progressive synagogues they sit together.

There are no representations of figures in the synagogue, as this would break the second of the Ten Commandments not to have images. Therefore, decoration is restricted to extracts from the scriptures or patterns.

Discussion activity

Read the second commandment below. As a whole class, discuss whether or not it matters if there are pictures of people or animals in a place of worship. Explain your opinion.

Beliefs and teachings

The second commandment

You shall not make for yourself an idol in the form of anything in heaven above or on the earth beneath or in the waters below. You shall not bow down to them or worship them.

Exodus 20:4–5

links

See page 103 to find out more about the dietary laws of Judaism.

See pages 46–47 to find out more about worship on the Sabbath.

Extension activity

The scroll (Sefer Torah) is 'dressed' in symbolic objects that link back to the robes of the Temple priests in Jerusalem before the Temple was destroyed in 70 CE.

Using the internet or a library, find out what the following features on the scroll represent:

- A breastplate
- Bells
- The mantle

Key terms

Ner tamid: eternal (everlasting) light above the Ark.

Bimah: a desk or platform for the reading of the Torah.

AQA Examiner's tip

Make sure that you are familiar with all the terms used to describe features within Jewish places of worship.

links

See page 97 to find out more about the Ten Commandments.

See pages 46–47 to find out more about Jewish worship.

Summary

You should now be able to describe and explain the symbolism of the exterior and interior features of Jewish places of worship.

1.8 Places of worship in Sikhism

■ Worship in Sikhism

Sikhs believe in only one God, whose teachings were given to them through the holy scripture, the Guru Granth Sahib. Sikhs believe that the best way to worship God is by following the Gurus, and living an honest life in which there is concern for others.

The place of worship for Sikhs is called the *gurdwara*, meaning 'doorway to the Guru'.

Worship in the home

Meditation is an important part of Sikh worship, as Sikhs believe that meditation helps to develop a deeper relationship with God. Meditation may take place in the gurdwara, but more frequently at home.

In the home, there are often pictures of the Ten Gurus, particularly the first one, Guru Nanak. Prayers are said every morning and evening. If Sikhs have a copy of the Guru Granth Sahib, this will be kept in a separate room.

■ The exterior of Sikh places of worship

A Sikh gurdwara is recognisable by the Sikh flag flying with the *nishan sahib* (the Sikh emblem). The nishan sahib symbolises all that Sikhs believe about God. The two outer crossed swords symbolise God's spiritual power. The ring of steel represents the unity of God, and the two-edged sword in the centre symbolises God's concern for truth and justice.

A purpose-built gurdwara will have four doors representing the four points of the compass to show that everyone is welcome. These are called the Door of Peace, the Door of Livelihood, the Door of Learning and the Door of Grace.

Worshippers remove their shoes before entering and so there will be a storage area for footwear.

> **Objectives**
> Describe the exterior and interior features of Sikh places of worship.
>
> Explain the symbolism of the exterior and interior of Sikh places of worship.

> **Key terms**
> **Gurdwara:** the Sikh place of worship. Literally 'the doorway to the Guru'.
> **Nishan sahib:** the Sikh emblem.

A *The Sikh flag*

> **Activity**
> 1. Draw and label the various parts of the nishan sahib, explaining their symbolic meaning.

B *The Golden Temple at Amritsar*

C *Sikhs praying before the Guru Granth Sahib inside a gurdwara*

The interior of Sikh places of worship

Worship takes place in a main hall called the Darbar Sahib. The focus of attention is the **Guru Granth Sahib**, which is placed on a raised platform called the **takht**. Above the takht is a canopy, the **palki**. The Guru Granth Sahib is covered with an expensive cloth when it is not being read. At night, it is kept in a room of its own. At the beginning of each day's worship, it is carried in procession into the main hall. Before the Guru Granth Sahib, money, flowers and food will be placed as offerings to God.

Worshippers sit on the floor at a level below the Guru Granth Sahib as a mark of respect. Although Sikhs show reverence for the Guru Granth Sahib, their reverence is not for the book itself but for the teachings from God within it. The book is a visible sign of God's presence.

Key terms

Guru Granth Sahib: collection of Sikh scriptures, collated by Guru Arjan and Guru Gobind Singh.

Takht: the throne where the Guru Granth Sahib is placed when it is open. The Five Takhts are places of authority in Sikhism. The Akal Takht (Throne of the Eternal) in Amritsar is the main one.

Palki: the canopy above the takht (raised platform) in a Sikh gurdwara.

Activity

2 Sikhs men and women worship together but sit in separate areas.

'If men and women are considered equal, then they should not have to sit separately during worship.' Do you agree? Give reasons for your answer, showing that you have thought about more than one point of view.

Around the wall there will be pictures of holy people, especially of Guru Nanak, the founder of Sikhism. A light is always burning in a gurdwara, to show that the Guru's light is always visible and is accessible to everyone at any time.

Activity

3 Describe and explain the features found in the interior of a Sikh gurdwara.

AQA Examiner's tip

Make sure that you are familiar with all the terms used to describe features within Sikh places of worship.

links

See pages 48–49 to find out more about Sikh worship.

See page 134 for a picture of Guru Nanak.

Summary

You should now be able to describe and explain the symbolism of the exterior and interior features of Sikh places of worship.

1.9 The value of religious buildings

> **Activity**
>
> 1. Look back at two of the religions whose places of worship are described on pages 12–23.
>   a. List the value of the buildings in each faith to an individual or the religion.
>   b. Compare your list with the points discussed in this section.

> **Objectives**
>
> Investigate why buildings are of value to an individual or the religion.

Places of worship as a way of expressing spirituality

The design of a place of worship may encourage some **spiritual** response from those viewing or using the building. It may encourage people to think about some aspect of life or faith. The symbolism of the building or its features may be important in conveying a message, or act as a reminder of past events within the history of the faith. For example, stained-glass windows may tell a story from the religion's scriptures.

> **Key terms**
>
> **Spiritual:** concerned with the mind or spirit, and/or religious matters, rather than the physical body; the opposite of material.

> **Case study**
>
> ### Stained-glass window: the Adoration of the Magi
>
> Most people attending church in the Middle Ages could not read, and one of the ways in which they were taught about the Christian faith was through pictures, such as those on stained-glass windows.
>
> In the example in the photograph, the three kings (the Magi) are bringing their gifts to the baby Jesus, who is sitting on his mother Mary's knee. The picture is reminding Christians that Jesus was special from the moment of his birth and is believed by them to be the Son of God.
>
> **A** Stained-glass window: the Adoration of the Magi

The value of buildings to an individual

A special building for worship can be very valuable to an individual, as going to a separate place will help them to focus on their faith. Also, attending a place of worship is a way of showing commitment to the faith.

> **links**
>
> If you need to check on the meaning of adoration, you can look it up in the Glossary at the back of this book.

The value of buildings to the religion

The kind of worship that takes place in the religion shapes the design of the building. This means that the people are able to come together and worship in what they believe to be the most helpful way for them. Buddhists do not believe in God, so it would not be appropriate for them to worship in a place in which God is held in deep respect. Similarly, Muslims and Jews do not believe that there should be representations of God and, therefore, could not worship within a Hindu temple with its display of statues and pictures of gods and goddesses. In Christianity, there are many different denominations with different beliefs about how worship should be performed. Therefore, each denomination requires different features within their buildings. For example, the Anglican, Roman Catholic, Orthodox and other churches baptise babies and have a font, but the Baptist Church baptises adults and needs a pool called a baptistery.

A special place where worship can take place also provides a sense of community. By coming together, the believers are able to realise that they are part of a much larger community.

B *A sunken pool with steps called a baptistery found in a Baptist church*

Do believers need a special building for worship?

Some believers think that it is better to worship at home and there is no need for a special building for worship. Others think that it is important to have a special building at which the community of believers can meet and worship together. Below are some of the reasons given by each group:

It is better to worship at home

- Individuals are able to have a one-to-one relationship with God.
- There will be no distractions and this will make it easier to pray and meditate.
- Individuals are able to worship as they wish without following a set pattern.
- Worship can take place at any time rather than at the set times of worship in a religious building.
- If God is everywhere then it is not necessary to go to a special building for worship.

It is better to worship in a religious building

- Prayers offered by a community of believers will be stronger.
- By following a leader of the worship, there is little risk of getting the worship wrong.
- By attending places of worship, individuals learn more about the teachings of their religion.
- A religious building can be designed as an appropriate place of worship for the religion.
- It helps to keep the faith of individuals alive when they worship alongside each other.
- The building itself can help individuals to feel closer to God.

links

See page 106 to find out more about baptism.

Discussion activity

In groups of four, discuss whether it is of greater value to a believer to worship at home or within a religious building. Explain your opinion.

AQA Examiner's tip

Make sure that you are able to give arguments for and against having a special building for worship.

Summary

You should now be able to explain and assess the value of a religious building to an individual and to the religion.

Activities

2 a Explain the value of a special building for worship to an individual.
   b Explain the value of a special building for worship to the religion.

3 'The building should be recognisable as a place of worship.' Do you agree? Give reasons for your answer, showing that you have thought about more than one point of view.

1.10 Places of worship in the community

■ The use and role in the community of places of worship

Besides being a place of regular acts of worship, the religious building often serves other functions in the community. These include:

- a place for religious ceremonies besides acts of worship, e.g. marriages
- a place for religious teaching
- a meeting place
- a community centre
- a place to hold social events
- a place to provide hospitality.

A place for religious ceremonies

Many religious buildings are used for other religious ceremonies to mark the rites of passage in a believer's life. These include ceremonies to mark the birth of a baby, initiation ceremonies, marriage ceremonies and funerals. Some mosques act as mortuaries, where the bodies of the dead are washed and stored until the funeral.

A place for religious teaching

The religious building is a place where the believers, both children and adults, can learn more about their faith.

The teaching of children

Children are often taught in special classes, and there may be special rooms or buildings in or near the religious building for this purpose. For example:

- Christians will often hold Sunday Schools where children will learn about their faith while their family attends a service in the church.
- Muslim children attend a madrassah each day, where they are taught about the religion and the Muslim way of life. They will learn to recite the Qur'an and may learn Arabic.
- Orthodox Jewish boys will attend classes to learn Hebrew ready for their initiation ceremony (Bar Mitzvah), in which they have to read a section of the Torah before the synagogue congregation.
- Sikh children attend music classes to learn traditional instruments.

The teaching of adults

Many religious buildings will have a library of books, which can be read by members of the faith to extend their knowledge and understanding of their religion. There may also be classes to prepare people for important events such as marriage, or entry into full membership of the faith, or to increase their awareness of what is expected of them as a believer. Special lectures on the teaching of the faith may be arranged. For example, there are often classes at a Buddhist temple to teach meditation.

Objectives

Investigate the other uses of religious buildings besides worship.

AQA Examiner's tip

You need to know the role of places of worship in the community, as well as how they are used for worship.

CO links

See pages 106–109 to find out more about the rites of passage within the religions that you are studying.

A A madrassah

A meeting place

After the act of worship, members of the congregation will often stay behind to talk with others who have attended the worship. Sometimes there will be tea, coffee and/or food available.

Meetings will be held in the building to decide important issues related to the religious community, or how fundraising and social events are to be organised.

A community centre

All the religions studied teach that it is an important part of worship to care for the less fortunate, and this is also an important use of religious buildings. One way in which the buildings can be used is to collect money to help those in need.

- Each year, some local Christian churches arrange an event called Christian Aid Week to support projects in the less-developed parts of the world.
- Many mosques provide meals for the elderly members of the community.

B *Fundraising activities were organised after the devastation caused by the 2004 tsunami in the Indian Ocean*

A place to hold social events

Believers are involved not only in acts of worship in their religious building but also in social events. For example, many Muslims get together at the mosque to break the fast each night during Ramadan.

There are often youth clubs held in rooms or separate buildings attached to the place of worship.

links
See page 86 to find out more about the Muslim celebration of the month of Ramadan.

A place to provide hospitality

A number of places of worship will show hospitality to visitors by offering food or refreshment. For example, all gurdwaras are open to everyone, regardless of race or religion. Every day, the **langar** serves vegetarian meals for the whole community and these are free to visitors. All members of the community contribute to the langar by donating food or money. Some gurdwaras provide overnight accommodation. Some places of worship offer a bed for the night or a hot meal to the homeless. An example from Christianity is the crypt of St George's Church in Leeds, which provides food and shelter to the homeless, asylum seekers and refugees.

Key terms
Langar: the dining hall of the gurdwara and the food served there. Literally 'Guru's kitchen' (Sikhism).

Activity
'It is wrong to hold social events in a place of worship.' Do you agree? Give reasons for your answer, showing that you have thought about more than one point of view.

Discussion activity
With a partner, in a small group or as a whole class, discuss the following statement: 'Religious buildings should only be used for worship.' Do you agree? Give reasons for your answer, showing that you have thought about more than one point of view.

Summary
You should now be able to explain different uses of religious buildings besides worship.

Assessment guidance

1

Places of worship – summary

With reference to at least **two** of the religions you have studied, for the examination you should now be able to:

✔ describe and explain the use of the home as a place of worship

✔ describe and explain the symbolism of the exterior of the buildings

✔ describe and explain the symbolism of the internal features of the buildings

✔ describe and explain the use and symbolism of the furnishings

✔ explain why there are religious buildings

✔ explain the use and role of religious buildings in the community

✔ evaluate whether or not it is right to spend money on religious buildings

✔ evaluate the value of buildings to an individual and to the religion.

Sample answer

1 Write an answer to the following examination question:

'A believer does not need to go to a special building to worship.'
Do you agree? Give reasons for your answer, showing that you have thought about more than one point of view. Refer to religious arguments in your answer.

(6 marks)

2 Read the following sample answer:

> I think that it is better to worship at home as God is everywhere and not just in a special building. If I worship at home, then I can worship God when I feel that I want to pray or meditate rather than having to wait for the set times at a religious building. I think that prayer is in the heart not in a building. The early followers of most faiths worshipped simply and so by worshipping at home I would be following their example. I find it easier to focus on my prayers and meditation at home without the distraction of other worshippers.
>
> Most believers would agree that there should be worship in the home, but would also want to take part in acts of worship in a special building. They think that faith is strengthened when you worship alongside people who share your beliefs. They also think that when they listen to a sermon they learn more about their faith, and are reminded of how they should live their life according to the teachings of their religion.
>
> Some believers who want special places of worship think that the building itself is a way of showing devotion to God or their religion. I do not agree as I think that God would want people to use the money to help the less fortunate rather than to spend it on a special place of worship.

3 With a partner, discuss the sample answer. This answer would be marked 6 out of 6 by the examiner. Why do you think that the examiner would give this answer full marks? Refer back to the mark scheme in the Introduction on page 7 (A02).

AQA Examination-style questions

1   Look at the photographs and answer the following questions.

   (a) (i)   Name **two** places of worship. *(2 marks)*
   (ii) For **each** of the **two** places of worship you have studied, explain briefly how you would have known from the outside of that building that it is a place of worship. *(3 marks)*

   > **AQA Examiner's tip:** Remember, you need to refer to the places of worship in at least two religions in this section of the examination.

   (b)   For **each** of the **two** places of religion you have studied, describe the inside of the place of worship. *(4 marks)*
   (c)   'It is better to pray in private than in public.' What do you think? Explain your opinion. *(3 marks)*
   (d)   'It is important to spend money on a place of worship.' Do you agree? Give reasons for your answer, showing that you have thought about more than one point of view. Refer to religious arguments in your answer. *(6 marks)*

   > **AQA Examiner's tip:** Remember that when you are given a statement and asked 'do you agree?' you must show what you think and the reasons why other people might take a different view. If your answer is one sided, you can only achieve a maximum of 4 marks. If you make no comment about religious belief or practice, you will achieve no more than 3 marks.

2 Worship

2.1 Worship

The word 'worship' comes from 'worth-ship', which means to attribute or give worth or value to something or someone. In most religions, it involves specific acts of praise, honour or devotion given to a supernatural being such as God, a god or goddess. Buddhists do not worship a supernatural being, although in Buddhism there are different forms of worship. These forms are directed to merit-making and escaping the cycle of birth, life, death and rebirth (samsara) to reach nibbana. In Mahayana Buddhism (practised in China, Japan and Tibet), worship takes the form of devotion to the Buddha and to Bodhisattvas. In Theravada Buddhism (practised in Burma, Thailand and elsewhere in southern Asia), formal public worship is not seen to be as important as private worship.

Worship may be performed individually or within a group, in the home or a special building constructed for worship or anywhere the worshipper believes is appropriate.

Worship practices differ between religions, but they usually include public and private acts of devotion, praying, reading from sacred writings, meditation, music and/or singing, sharing food, listening to a sermon or talk and taking part in celebrations (e.g. festivals) and rituals. Worship may take place at any time, but many faiths have a particular day each week set aside for worship activities. Worshippers often use items to symbolise different beliefs or as aids to help them concentrate while worshipping.

Why worship?

Buddhists, Hindus and Sikhs believe that one of the functions of worship is that it results in positive merit (or good kamma or karma). Buddhists believe that it helps a person purify themselves and reach enlightenment. Although they look up to the Buddha, they do not think that he was a god, so Buddhist worship is designed to benefit the worshipper and lead to the ultimate aim of reaching nibbana. The Vedas scriptures encourage Hindus to worship the One Supreme God, but this might be done through focusing on his many representatives, including a variety of gods (devas) and goddesses (devis). By pleasing the gods or goddesses, it is hoped that the wishes of the worshipper will be granted and merit will be obtained.

The main purpose of worship for Sikhs is to praise God. Public worship also gives the opportunity to remember the Gurus and to share in food, which symbolises the importance of equality.

Christians, Muslims and Jews regard worshipping God as an essential part of their faith. Christians believe that worship enables them to thank God, ask forgiveness for sin and respond to the love of Jesus

> **Objectives**
> Understand what is meant by worship and why people worship.

> **Key terms**
> **Worship:** acts of religious praise, honour or devotion.
> **Devotion:** religious worship.
> **Merit-making:** the process of deserving, earned by service or performance.

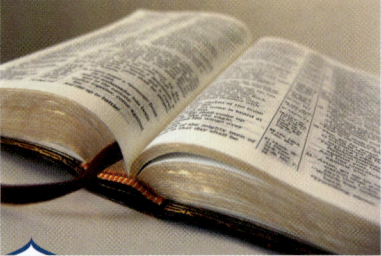

A Sacred writings are used in worship

links
See page 75 for a definition of the term 'nibbana', or you can look it up in the Glossary at the back of this book.

Look back to Chapter 1 for details of the special places of worship for each religion.

as shown through his death on the cross. They teach that Jesus' sacrifice enabled the relationship with God, which had been broken by sin, to be restored, bringing salvation and eternal life, and this deserves a response. Christians believe that all creation reflects God's glory and people are commanded to worship:

> ❝ Through Jesus, therefore, let us continually offer to God a sacrifice of praise – the fruit of lips that confess his name. ❞
>
> Hebrews 13:15

The Qur'an teaches Muslims that humans were created for the purpose or function of worshipping Allah:

> ❝ I did not create the jinns and the humans except to worship Me alone. ❞
>
> Qur'an 51:56

Jews are also taught to worship the one whom they regard as the true God. To worship another god would cause God to be upset and angry:

> ❝ Do not worship any other god, for the LORD, whose name is Jealous, is a jealous God. ❞
>
> Exodus 34:14

Jews see worship as giving to God, not as getting. They do not worship to receive but to respond to God's love:

> ❝ Give thanks to the Lord, for he is good; his love endures forever. ❞
>
> Psalms 107:1

B Hands raised in worship and praise

AQA Examiner's tip

For the religions you are studying, make sure that you can explain the function and value of worship.

Discussion activity

With a partner, in a small group or as a whole class, discuss the purpose and value of worship. Explain your opinion.

Activities

1. Explain what is meant by 'worship' and 'obtaining merit'.

2. 'The main purpose of worship is to thank God for creation.' Do you agree? Give reasons for your answer, showing that you have thought about more than one point of view.

Summary

You should now be able to explain what is meant by worship and the value of worship to those who do it.

2.2 Days of worship

Days of worship

Some religions have a special day each week when followers are encouraged to attend public worship. Some religious believers say that without the discipline of a special day set aside, there is a danger that every day would become the same and worship would get neglected. For example, some Christians in Britain have campaigned to keep Sunday special as a holy day, set aside for family, rest and worship rather than forcing thousands to work. Others argue that worship should take place every day or else religion is forgotten about on the other six days of the week. Atheists (non-believers) do not see the point in any form of worship.

Buddhism

Buddhists do not have a special day of the week that must be kept sacred, but many attend the temples and other places of worship on festival days.

Christianity

To most Christians, Sunday is a special day of worship, although some will say that they 'worship' every day. The New Testament does not specify any particular day for worship and leaves it open to the individual.

Most Christians have chosen Sunday, the first day of the week, as a day for worship for two main reasons:

1. It is the day they believe Jesus rose from the dead. Sunday as the day of the resurrection enables Christians to give thanks and celebrate their risen saviour in Sunday worship.
2. Sunday is the day when Christians believe the Holy Spirit came to the disciples in Jerusalem at Pentecost. Many celebrate this event, when the disciples heard a sound like a mighty rushing wind and saw something that looked like tongues of fire, as the birth of the Church.

Hinduism

Hindus do not have a special day for worship, but most practising Hindus perform puja (worship) once or twice a day. This takes place either in the home or in the mandir (temple).

Islam

Every day is a day of worship for Muslims, as the second pillar of Islam (salah) states that Muslims must pray five times a day, every day. Friday is, however, regarded as the Muslim holy day when many gather in the mosque for special prayers (**Jumu'ah**). Muslims believe that Allah created Adam on a Friday and any devotional acts done on Fridays are thought to gain a higher reward. It is the duty of Muslim men to attend Jumu'ah, join in the congregational prayer and listen to the sermons. Women may choose whether or not to be there, but it is considered to be spiritually highly beneficial.

> **Objectives**
> Know about days of worship and why they were chosen.
> Understand the importance of days of worship.

A *Christians believe Jesus rose on a Sunday*

> **Key terms**
> **Jumu'ah:** weekly communal salah performed after midday on a Friday (Islam).

links

See page 86 to find out about the Five Pillars of Islam.

Chapter 2 Worship 33

B Muslims at Friday prayers

Judaism

Jews observe the fourth commandment (Exodus 20:8–11), which is to keep the Sabbath Day holy. It is referred to as **Shabbat**. The special status of the seventh day of the week is also given in the first book of the Torah:

> *And God blessed the seventh day and made it holy, because on it he rested from all the work of creating that he had done.*
>
> Genesis 2:3

Jewish days start at sunset in the evening and finish the following evening at sunset. So Shabbat is observed from sundown on Friday until the appearance of three stars in the sky on Saturday night. It is seen as a precious day of rest that may be spent with the family and worshipping God.

Sikhism

Sikhs do not have a particular holy day each week. They are taught that each moment should be considered holy and life itself should be considered as an act of devotion. In Britain, most Sikh families worship in the gurdwara on a Sunday.

Key terms

Shabbat (Sabbath): holy day of the week; day of spiritual renewal beginning at sunset on Friday and continuing to nightfall on Saturday (Judaism).

AQA Examiner's tip

Be aware that Saturday is the seventh day of the week and Sunday is the first day of the week. It is a common fault to say that Sunday is the seventh day.

Activities

1. Explain the importance of a day of worship to Christians, Jews and Muslims, and why the days were chosen.
2. Explain why Buddhists, Hindus and Sikhs do not have a particular holy day each week.
3. 'Sundays should be kept special.' What do you think? Explain your opinion.

Discussion activity

With a partner, in a small group or as a whole class, discuss the advantages and disadvantages of having a day of worship each week. Explain your opinion.

Summary

You should now be able to explain the importance of a special day of worship to some religions and explain how it was chosen.

2.3 Aids to worship and prayer

Aids to worship

Aids to worship may be used for both private and public worship.

Singing bowl

In the Himalayan region some Buddhists use a singing bowl. Made of metal, it makes a sound when tapped with a wooden stick that assists in meditation and is believed to release the mantras.

Mandalas

Mandalas are used in both Buddhism and Hinduism. Mandalas may be in different forms, for example a sacred circle or circular diagram, but each represents geometric designs of the universe. Buddhists and Hindus believe that this symbol serves as a collection point for universal forces, and so it is used in meditation. Inside the circle are often very detailed pictures or geometric patterns, which are thought to help with concentration. The idea is mentally to enter the mandala and go to its centre, which symbolically enables a person to be guided through the universe to a place of reality and enlightenment. In Buddhism, different colours are used with symbolic meanings. Red represents the Buddha's compassion, white his purity and blue the truth of his teaching.

Rangolis

Hindus decorate the outside of their homes with rangolis. This is a form of sand painting using finely ground white powder and colours. The beauty of the paintings, which are particularly created at the Diwali festival, spreads joy and happiness all around.

Yad

When reading the Torah scrolls, Jews use a yad to point to the place on the parchment so the reader does not lose their place. This enables the sacred scroll to be kept clean and undamaged. A yad is usually like a rod with a small hand and index finger pointing from it and it is often made of silver.

Icons and candles

The Eastern Orthodox Church uses icons (pictures of Jesus or the saints) to help focus during devotions. The saints are not worshipped, but are held in high esteem. Several denominations use candles. Christians also use a crucifix or cross to help them to remember the sacrifice of Jesus and his resurrection from the dead. Incense may be used to symbolise God's presence in worship, and hymn books might be used when singing sacred songs (hymns).

Objectives

Know about the use of aids to worship.

Understand the types of prayer used by Christians and others.

Key terms

Mandala: a circular sacred diagram (Buddhism and Hinduism).

Rangolis: artistic patterns made with different coloured grains (rice, lentils). It forms part of Hindu celebrations.

Yad: a pointer used when reading the Torah scrolls.

links

See page 112 to find out more about the Hindu Diwali festival.

A *Saying Grace before meals*

Prayer

Prayer or meditation takes many forms. For example, there are many different types of prayer used by Christians or Jews. These include:

- adoration – praising God for his greatness and acknowledging dependence on him
- thanksgiving – thanking God for his goodness and provision, for example saying Grace before meals
- confession – admitting sin and asking God for forgiveness and mercy
- intercession – praying for those who need God's help or support
- petition/supplication – asking God for spiritual and physical needs for themselves
- meditation – waiting for God to speak or resting in his presence, for example by Quakers at their meetings as they sit in silence.

Research activity

Using a Bible, find out how Jesus taught his disciples to pray (Luke 11:2–4).

B Thousands worshipping in the open air

Case study: Prayer and success

A Church in Seoul, South Korea, has a membership of over 830 000. Yoido Full Gospel Church was founded by Dr David Yonggi Cho in 1958 and has seen phenomenal growth from around 30 members to become the world's largest single Church. Despite satellite churches having been built in other parts of Seoul, up to nine services are held each Sunday in order to accommodate all the people. Yonggi Cho puts the success of his Church down to fasting and prayer. Thousands attend the church at 4.30am and pray before going to work, and on Friday night over 10 000 people pray aloud together throughout the night, from 10.00pm to 4.30am. In 1973, the Church started taking people to the Osanri Prayer Mountain and built facilities for 10 000 people to pray. Each year, over 1 million people visit the mountain to pray.

Extension activity

Using the internet, find out more about worship in the Yoido Full Gospel Church before doing the Discussion activity.

Discussion activity

With a partner, in a small group or as a whole class, discuss the case study by trying to imagine the noise, the fervour, the excitement, the atmosphere and the problems of a Church the size of Yoido. Do you think that something like this could happen in Britain? Give reasons for your answer.

Activities

1. Name **two** aids used in worship and explain their uses.
2. Explain the different types of prayer used in Christianity.
3. 'Prayer or meditation is the most important form of worship.' Do you agree? Give reasons for your answer, showing that you have thought about more than one point of view.

Summary

You should now be able to explain the use of aids for worship and the different types of prayer used by Christians and others.

2.4 Prayer aids

One of the most important parts of worship is prayer. To help focus in prayer, some worshippers use prayer aids.

Prayer beads

Buddhists, Christians, Hindus and Muslims use prayer beads to help them keep count of the repetitions of prayers, chants or devotions. Some Sikhs use **mala beads** for naam jap (reciting God's name) or they use a prayer string made of wool with 99 knots.

Mahayana Buddhists use japa malas, which have 108 beads or a number that can be multiplied to make that total, such as 27 or 54. In Tibetan Buddhism, malas usually have 108 beads. Some malas have three large beads to represent the Buddha, the dharma (his teachings) and the sangha, or Buddhist community.

Hindus were the first to use japa mala prayer beads. Hindus use them to count the number of **mantras** that have been said and when repeating the name of a god or goddess. The number of beads may be 108 or a number divisible by nine. Traditionally, the mala is held in the right hand, draped over the middle finger, and the thumb is used to flick from one bead to the next as a mantra is said.

Roman Catholic Christians use Rosary beads when praying the Rosary. The prayers follow a repeated sequence of saying the Lord's Prayer, followed by the Hail Mary prayer 10 times and a single praying of 'Glory Be to the Father'. During each of these sequences, the worshipper meditates on one of the 15 Mysteries of the Rosary (events in the lives of Jesus and the Virgin Mary). The fingers are moved along the beads as the prayers are recited, enabling full concentration on praying. There are various versions of the Rosary beads, including a ring and a bracelet. The beads are made of different materials including glass, plastic, wood or precious materials such as silver or gold.

Muslim prayer beads are called tasbih or misbah. Each bead represents one of the 99 known names of Allah. Sometimes 33 beads are used, with each bead being used three times. Most are wooden, but other materials such as amber, ivory, olive seeds, pearls or plastic are also used.

Prayer wheels and flags

Prayer wheels, used in particular by Tibetan Buddhists, consist of a spindle usually made from metal, wood or leather containing mantras and Buddhist symbols. The prayer is said orally before and after the wheel is turned, or it is believed that no merit is obtained. As the wheel is turned clockwise, smoothly and calmly, the mantra is repeated orally so each revolution brings merit equal to reading the mantra aloud by as many times as it is written on the prayer scroll.

Mantras are also written on flags that are hung up in a line. Tibetan Buddhists believe that the prayer is repeated each time the flag moves in the wind. Sets of five-colour flags are arranged in the order of

Objectives
Find out about aids used to assist a worshipper in prayer.

Key terms
Mala beads: a string of beads used as a prayer aid.

Mantra: a short prayer/chant repeated as an aid to meditation, such as Om Mani Padme Hum in Buddhism.

A Buddhist mala beads

links
Look back to page 34 to remind yourself of other aids to worship.

B Muslim father and son holding prayer beads

C *Tibetan Buddhist prayer flags*

yellow, green, red, white and blue (from left to right or from bottom to top). The colours represent the elements: earth, water, fire, cloud and sky.

Mezuzah and tefillin

The most important Jewish prayer is the Shema, which is repeated in synagogue services and is the final prayer many Jews say at night. To remind them, it is written on a small scroll and placed in a small box called a mezuzah, which is fixed to a doorpost and touched by those who enter the house.

Male Jews may wear **tefillin** (also called phylacteries) during weekday morning prayer services. Tefillin include two black leather boxes containing the Shema and other texts written on small scrolls.

Activities

1. Choose **three** aids used in prayer. Describe them and explain how they are used.

2. 'All religious believers should use prayer aids.' Do you agree? Give reasons for your answer, showing that you have thought about more than one point of view.

Discussion activity

With a partner, in a small group or as a whole class, discuss why many religious believers use aids to help them pray. Give reasons for your answer.

Summary

You should now be able to describe and explain the use of various aids for prayer and evaluate their importance.

Research activity

Using the internet or a library, find out more about at least **one** of the following:
- Mala beads
- Rosary beads
- Tasbih
- Prayer wheels and flags
- Tefillin

Key terms

Tefillin: two small leather boxes fastened by straps to the forehead and arm for morning prayers on week days.

links

See page 88 for more on the Shema.

AQA Examiner's tip

Make sure that you know the technical terms for the different aids for prayer used by believers in the religion(s) you are studying.

2.5 Buddhist worship

Worship in the home

Most Buddhist devotions for the laity (ordinary people – not monks or nuns) take place in the home. Many have a shrine room, which usually has an image of the Buddha, flowers, candles, a tray of food offerings and an incense burner. The form of worship differs according to the type of Buddhism of the worshipper, but often begins every morning and evening with the recitation of the Three Refuges and the Five Moral Precepts. Buddhists do not feel they have to perform this worship, but merit or good kamma is earned by doing so. Worship includes prayer and meditation. Requests may be made for a long life or a good rebirth, for example.

Buddhists meditate to follow the Buddha's example, with the aim of achieving enlightenment. Meditation is an attempt to clear the mind of all thoughts so that negative ones such as anger, greed and ignorance can be replaced with positive ones such as peace and tranquillity. There are different types of Buddhist meditation including **samatha** and **vipassana**. Samatha meditation is designed to develop the ability to focus the attention on one object or idea. Those meditating may concentrate on such things as their breath (anapana), loving-kindness (metta), a scripture passage, a religious picture or a mantra. This enables their minds to become calm, alert and focused.

Vipassana meditation is aimed at developing insight and wisdom through seeing and understanding the true nature of things. Samatha meditation is used to build up to this.

Buddhists might use the Tripitaka (the Three Baskets) when meditating. These are three groups of sacred writings, which focus on the rules of behaviour for monks, the Buddha's teachings and Buddhist philosophy.

Worship in the temple

For many Buddhists, worship (puja) in the temple is not as important as worship in the home, but on full-moon days and festivals many visit the monasteries or temples. Before entering the shrine room, they will remove their shoes as a sign of respect. Theravada Buddhists take gifts of flowers, candles, rosaries and incense to present to statues of the Buddha (rupas). Any formal service consists of chanting of Buddhist beliefs and scriptures. Mahayana Buddhists also take gifts, but devotion is also shown to **bodhisattas**. Usually worship begins by reciting the Three Refuges. A bell is used to inform people when to begin the next stage in puja or meditation. Candles are lit as a symbol of the Buddha's teaching showing people the right way to live to reach enlightenment. Flowers are a reminder of anicca (impermanence) as they fade and die. Food is place in bowls as an offering and incense sticks are placed on the shrine. The sweet smell spreads through the room, symbolising the Buddha's teaching spreading through the world. **Bhikkhus** or **bhikkhuni** may read sutras (sacred texts) or a monk might preach a sermon explaining the practical application of a scripture to everyday life. Afterwards, it is customary to socialise with the monks or to continue meditating.

> **Objectives**
>
> Investigate how Buddhists worship at home and in the temple.
>
> Explain the forms of meditation and the role of the sangha and bhikkhus.

> **Key terms**
>
> **Samatha:** a state of concentrated calmness achieved by meditation.
>
> **Vipassana (vipashyana):** reaching an insight into the true nature of things through meditation.
>
> **Bodhisatta (Bodhisattva):** someone who is destined to become enlightened but postpones this so they can help others to achieve it as well.
>
> **Bhikkhu (bhikshu):** a fully ordained Buddhist monk.
>
> **Bhikkhuni (bhishuni):** a fully ordained Buddhist nun.

A A Buddhist shrine in Thailand

B *Buddhist monks*

links

See pages 96–97 for more on the Three Refuges and the Five Moral Precepts, and page 125 for more on the Tripitaka.

Buddhists consider the **sangha** as the best place to advance towards enlightenment, and it is the Buddhist community that is responsible for advancing and spreading teachings of the Buddha.

Key terms

Sangha: the community of bhikkhus and bhikkunis.

Discussion activity

With a partner, in a small group or as a whole class, discuss which you think is the most important for Buddhists – private or public worship. Give reasons for your answer, showing that you have thought about more than one point of view.

Extension activity

Using the internet or a library, find out more about the role of the sangha and bhikkhus/bhikkhuni in worship.

Activities

1. Explain the difference between samatha and vipassana meditation.

2. Explain the items used by Buddhists at their home shrine or in the temple, and their symbolism.

3. 'The only way to reach enlightenment is to become a Buddhist monk.' Do you agree? Give reasons for your answer, showing that you have thought about more than one point of view.

AQA Examiner's tip

You are not expected to know about the difference between Theravada and Mahayana Buddhism, but examples from either tradition of their practices and beliefs will help you to answer questions.

Summary

You should now be able to understand and describe the importance of Buddhist worship in the home and in the temple. You should also be able to explain the forms of meditation and the role of the sangha and bhikkhus.

2.6 Christian worship

Worship in the home

Many Christians have a quiet time that they spend each day alone with God. This may involve reading Bible notes and a Bible passage and studying/meditating upon it. Part of the time may be spent praying to God or singing choruses or hymns. Some have family devotions when parents teach their children about the faith and God is recognised as the centre of family life. Stories from the Bible or of Christian leaders may be shared. Grace is said before meals to thank God for his provision, and other prayers may be said at the beginning and end of the day.

Public worship

Christian leaders such as bishops, priests, vicars, ministers and pastors have a leading role to play in Christian worship. There are many different Christian denominations and styles of worship and the exact role of the leaders varies. Often, they are responsible for leading the prayers and preaching the sermons, and in some churches they may lead all the worship. In other churches, musicians may lead the singing and there may be more participation by members of the congregation.

Types of Christian worship include liturgical worship. This is a set form of worship, quite often with a formal ritual based around the sacraments, for example **Holy Communion**. Usually a special book is used that enables the congregation to follow the service and read responses when prompted. An organ often provides music, traditional hymns are sung and the priest will give a talk or sermon based on a biblical passage.

> **Objectives**
>
> Understand some of the ways that Christians worship in the home and in church.
>
> Understand how and why Christians celebrate Holy Communion and its importance as a central act of worship.

> **Extension activity**
>
> Using the internet or a library, find out more about how Christian leaders lead worship.

> **Key terms**
>
> **Holy Communion:** a service of thanksgiving in which the sacrificial death and resurrection of Jesus is celebrated using bread and wine.

A *A priest preaching a sermon*

A lively and joyful type of non-liturgical worship (where there is no set pattern) is the charismatic form of worship. It is characterised by lots of singing of mainly modern worship songs led by a church music group consisting of guitars, drums, keyboards, etc. Worshippers may dance, wave flags, break into spontaneous prayer, speak in tongues (language given by the Holy Spirit), raise their hands in the air in worship, prophesy, give testimonies (share what Christianity means to them) and pray for people to be healed. Other churches may combine some elements of liturgical and non-liturgical worship, and alternative forms are being developed all the time. Youth services may be held that are focused on young people and may include multi-sensory experiences using video, projection and lighting, drama, crafts, games and quizzes and talks rather than sermons.

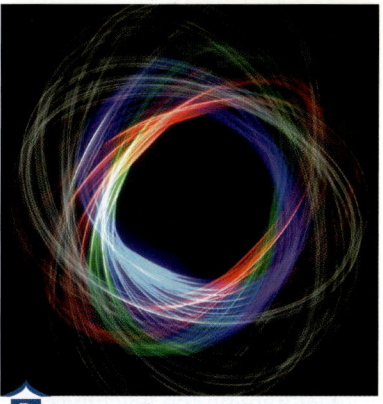

B *Many youth services have become a multi-sensory experience*

Holy Communion

Holy Communion is regarded as the central act of Christian worship in most denominations, although some, like the Society of Friends (Quakers) and The Salvation Army, do not celebrate it. There are many names given to this sacrament including the Eucharist, Mass, Divine Liturgy, the Lord's Supper and the Breaking of Bread. It commemorates the Last Supper of Jesus before his crucifixion (Matthew 26:26–8, Mark 14:22–4 and Luke 22:17–20) and includes eating bread (to represent Christ's broken body) and drinking wine (to represent his blood). There has been controversy between Christians over whether the consecrated bread and wine changes into the real presence of Jesus (the Roman Catholic view called transubstantiation) or whether Holy Communion is celebrated chiefly to remember Jesus' sacrifice on the cross (the view of most Protestants). In some denominations, Holy Communion is celebrated every Sunday, in others less frequently. Most Christians believe it is very important to celebrate Holy Communion because Jesus asked his followers to do this in memory of him.

C *A priest at Holy Communion*

Research activity

Using the internet or a library, find out more about how Holy Communion is celebrated in the different Christian denominations. For example, Roman Catholic, Eastern Orthodox, Anglican, Baptist or Methodist. Record your findings.

Discussion activity

With a partner, in a small group or as a whole class, discuss why you think that Jesus, as he offered them bread and wine, gave his followers the instruction to 'do this in remembrance of me' (Luke 22:19). Make notes on the key points to use as examples in your examination.

Activities

1. Describe how Christians may worship in the home and in church.
2. Explain the role of Christian leaders in worship.
3. 'Christian worship should always be lively and joyful.' Do you agree? Give reasons for your answer, showing that you have thought about more than one point of view.

AQA Examiner's tip

Be prepared to evaluate whether or not Holy Communion is the most important Christian form of worship.

Summary

You should now be able to describe how Christians worship in the home and in church and explain the importance of the service of Holy Communion.

2.7 Hindu worship

Worship in the home

For most Hindus, worship at home is more important than temple worship as it is performed daily. The five daily obligations or duties are:

1. Worship god daily (Deva Yagna).
2. Study the Vedas and other scriptures (Brahma Yagna).
3. Meditate on the teachings of important Hindus (Pitri Yagna).
4. Provide food for those in need (Bhuta Yagna).
5. Treat guests with love, respect and reverence (Nara Yagna).

Most Hindus have a shrine room in their homes, which might consist of a statue, photo or images of a god or goddess (murti).

Devout Hindus may take part in the **havan** or fire sacrifice each morning and evening and on special occasions such as a birth, wedding or festival. First, the worshipper bathes to purify themselves and then they make an offering to the fire god Agni in their household fire.

The second type of puja (worship) may take place at any time. Food or drink is offered to the shrine and mantras are said. The items used for worship are put on an **arti** tray, including an incense stick, flowers, fruit, ghee lamp, kum-kum powder, milk, rice-grains, turmeric powder and water. Family members may pray alone or together and may use a mala as they repeat the name of the murti while saying the word **Om (Aum)**. This sacred word represents the first three Vedas (Hindu holy books), the three worlds (earth, atmosphere and heaven) and the Hindu Trimurti (Brahma, Vishnu and Shiva). The symbol is written on the tongues of children in honey when they are born. Puja is seen as linking the worshipper's life to a deity, but the way a person lives is seen as vitally important:

> *But those who always strive to do good, and who are free from every inclination to do wrong, truly worship me.*
>
> *Bhagavad Gita 7.28*

Research activity

Using the internet or a library, find out more about why Hindus practise yoga and record your findings.

Objectives

Know and explain the five daily obligations.

Know and understand the ceremonies and rituals performed in the home and in the mandir.

Key terms

Havan: ceremony in which offerings of rice and ghee are made into fire.

Arti (arati): a welcoming ceremony in which items such as lamps or incense are offered to the deity or saintly people.

Om (Aum): the sacred sound and symbol that represents Brahman. It is used in mantras as part of Hindu worship.

links

Look back to page 16 to see a picture of the symbol Om.

A *Shrine of Lakshmi, goddess of wealth*

Worship in the mandir or temple

A priest (pandit) and his helpers lead temple worship. Often this involves early morning, midday, late-afternoon and evening puja. In the morning, the bell is rung to wake the gods, the deities are bathed and dressed, and flowers, incense and food are offered at the shrine. During worship, the congregation sits on the floor facing the shrine. Congregational worship involves singing hymns (**bhajans**) or listening to musicians play a song of praise (**kirtan**) and sometimes listening to a lecture based on scripture (**pravachan**). Havan is offered to the fire god and the priest places wood into a fire altar and sets it alight. As prayers are said, ghee is poured into the fire. Then the arti tray is passed in front of the deity. Worshippers put money on the tray and receive prashad (a mixture of sugar, dried fruits and nuts).

B A Hindu priest conducting puja in an Indian temple

Case study

Shri Swaminarayan Mandir

The largest Hindu temple in Britain is the BAPS Shri Swaminarayan Mandir (or Neasden Temple), which was opened in north-west London in 1995 at a cost of over £12m. Sadhus (holy men) wake the murtis before sunrise and prepare them for the Mangala Arti (the first of five 'arti' prayers that take place during the day). This involves a prayer being recited to music while the sadhus wave a lighted lamp in front of the murtis. After this, the deities are offered food and are bathed and the shrine doors are shut. The shrine is reopened between 9.00am and 11.00am for the second arti, then again at 11.45am for the midday arti. Between 4.00pm and 6.30pm is the fourth arti and the final one is at 7.00pm. After this, the deities are dressed in their night attire. With lights dimmed, soft music is played to send the deities to sleep.

Key terms

Bhajan: a Hindu hymn or song.

Kirtan: songs of praise usually accompanied by instruments.

Pravachan: a lecture based on the sacred texts.

Activities

1. Explain how Hindus worship in the home and in the mandir.

2. 'Worship in the home is far more important to Hindus than worship in the temple.' Do you agree? Give reasons for your answer, showing that you have thought about more than one point of view.

Discussion activity

With a partner, in a small group or as a whole class, discuss the five daily obligations. What duties do you think everyone should perform each day? Make notes on the opinions given, and the reasons for them.

Summary

You should now be able to describe and explain Hindu worship in the home and in the mandir.

AQA Examiner's tip

Be prepared to explain Hindu forms of worship in the home and in the mandir.

2.8 Muslim worship

Worship in the home

From birth, a Muslim child is brought up to learn the Qur'an and the Five Pillars of Islam. Words from the Qur'an are whispered in the baby's ear as soon as possible after birth. Homes have texts from the holy book on the walls and children are encouraged to learn prayers. Parents teach the children the rules about worship and prayer, and both the Qur'an and the Hadith (sayings of the prophet Muhammad) are studied. Mothers do not have to attend the mosque for the Friday Jumu'ah prayers (see page 32) and will often stay at home and pray with the children.

Salah is very important as it is the second pillar of Islam and is performed five times a day at set times – between dawn and sunrise, just after midday, in the afternoon, after sunset and in the evening. Prayer five times a day is an instruction from Allah given through Muhammad. It is seen as enabling the worshippers to stand before Allah to praise and thank him and to ask for guidance. Prayer may be done anywhere in the home, in the mosque or in any clean place. Most Muslims have their own prayer mat, which they use if needed.

Worship in the mosque

Praying together is regarded as having more value spiritually than praying alone, and being together strengthens the brotherhood (ummah) of Islam. Prayer times are announced from the minaret (tower of the mosque). The man who gives the call to prayer (the Adhan) is called the muezzin. The imam, a man who has been chosen because of his knowledge of the Qur'an, leads salah. Many imams have

Objectives

Understand the importance of salah (prayer) in Islam.

Know about private and public Muslim worship.

A Worshipping in the home

Key terms

Salah: prayer to and worship of Allah, performed under the conditions set by the Prophet Muhammad. The second pillar of Islam.

Imam: a person who leads communal prayer.

B Muslims at prayer

learned the whole Qur'an by heart and they lead the congregation through the performing actions and movements of the **rak'ahs** and preach the Jumu'ah sermon on Fridays, using words from the Qur'an. Women are not allowed to perform this role.

Before prayers, Muslims are required to prepare and focus by performing **wudu**. For Sunni Muslims, wudu consists of washing the hands, mouth, nose, face, arms, forehead and hair, ears and feet three times each in that order. Shia Muslims wash their face first, followed by their arms, and then use the moisture to wipe their head and feet. If water is not available, they are instructed to wipe their hands and face with clean sand.

Before entering the mosque, Muslims remove their shoes and sit on the carpeted floor facing the Ka'aba in Makkah. The direction of Makkah is indicated by a niche on a wall (known as the qiblah wall) and the worshippers sit in line. Women may attend the mosque but, in order not to detract the focus from Allah, sit either at the back behind the men or in a separate room.

Muslims pray by completing the rak'ahs whilst reciting sections from the Qur'an. This is done in unison following the actions of the imam who is at the front of the mosque with his back to the congregation. A set number of rak'ahs are performed at each prayer time, consisting of standing, bowing, kneeling and prostrating on the floor. Afterwards, personal prayers (du'a) may be said.

Key terms

- **Rak'ahs (rakas):** actions made during salah consisting of recitations, standing, bowing and prostration.
- **Wudu (wuzu):** ablutions – ritual washing before prayer.

Research activity

Using the internet or a library, find out the English translation of what Muslims repeat during salah and work out why these words are important to them.

AQA Examiner's tip

Make sure that you can explain the key elements in preparing and taking part in Muslim worship.

Discussion activity

With a partner, in a small group or as a whole class, discuss whether or not it helps religious believers to have a set time to pray and worship and a set routine to follow. Explain your opinion.

Extension activity

Using the internet or a library, find out what the muezzin says in order to encourage the faithful to pray. Record your findings.

Activities

1. a Explain the importance of prayer to Muslims.
   b Describe how Muslims perform salah in the mosque, including the role of the imam and the use of sacred texts.

2. 'Salah is the only way to become close to Allah.' Do you agree? Give reasons for your answer, showing that you have thought about more than one point of view.

Summary

You should now be able to explain the importance of salah and Jumu'ah prayers to Muslims. You should also now know and understand how salah is performed, how Muslims worship at home and in the mosque and who is involved in these prayers.

2.9 Jewish worship

Worship in the home

Jews are encouraged to pray three times each day (morning, afternoon and evening). These include prayers of thanksgiving, praise and petition (asking God for things) and are set out in the Jewish prayer book (siddur). Extra prayers are said during Shabbat (Sabbath) and special holy days. The home is vital for maintaining strong family links and teaching the traditions of Judaism, and many say that Jewish life is a form of worship in itself. This is because of the emphasis on a detailed code of conduct centring on the celebration of Shabbat, at home and in the synagogue. Shabbat celebrates the creation of the world and is kept special in obedience to the commandment 'Remember the Sabbath day by keeping it holy' (*Exodus* 20:8).

Shabbat lasts from Friday sunset until sunset on Saturday. During the Friday, the mother makes preparations for the Shabbat celebrations. The house is cleaned and tidied, the table is laid with the best crockery and food is prepared. At dusk, at the start of the meal, the mother lights two candles, prays, and welcomes in Shabbat, moving her arms towards the light.

The father blesses the bread (challah), which is plaited. This is sprinkled with salt and represents the double portion of manna that the Children of Israel received each Friday while in the wilderness during the Exodus. No work is done on Shabbat and it is celebrated as a day of rest, family time and worship. The father says the Kiddush (blessing) over a cup of wine, verses are repeated about the Sabbath and creation, the children are blessed and the meal eaten.

Saturday afternoon is spent studying the Torah, telling stories from Jewish history and enjoying the company of the family. At the end of Shabbat, the Havdalah ceremony takes place, separating Shabbat from the other six days of the week. Blessings are said over sweet-smelling spices, a special plaited candle and a cup of wine.

Worship in the synagogue

On Shabbat, a service is held in the synagogue on Friday before the ceremony to welcome in Shabbat in the home, but the main act of worship for Orthodox and Reform Jews starts at around 10.00am on the Saturday. The Hebrew language is used the most in an Orthodox service, and the least in a Reform one. A **rabbi** leads the services and a cantor (chazan) sings and leads the congregation in song. In an Orthodox synagogue, the women sit upstairs in the balcony with children under the age of 13. Men sit in the main body of the synagogue to form the minyan (at least 10 men over the age of 13, without whom the full service cannot take place). In Reform and Liberal synagogues, men and women sit together.

During the service, the Psalms are read and the scrolls (Sefer Torah) are taken from the Ark for the reading. This happens on three occasions each week – Monday, Thursday and Saturday. The Torah scroll is shown great respect as it is paraded around the synagogue covered

Objectives

Know how Jews worship in the home and in the synagogue.

Understand the importance of Shabbat.

Know how the Torah is used and the role of leaders in worship.

A *The mother welcomes in Shabbat*

Key terms

Rabbi: a Jewish religious leader and teacher.

B *Torah scroll*

Chapter 2 Worship 47

links

Look back to page 33 to remind yourself of the fourth commandment.

C A rabbi leading worship in the synagogue

with its mantle, breastplate, bells and crown. Those present touch the scroll with their tallits (prayer shawl), which they then kiss, before it is carried on to the bimah (raised platform). There are set readings for each week, and prayers are said for the nation and Israel. The scrolls are returned to the Ark while blessings are said, and the rabbi then preaches a sermon. More prayers are said and the Hymn of Glory is chanted before the end of the service.

AQA Examiner's tip

Be aware that there are different forms of Judaism, e.g. Orthodox, Reform and Liberal, and that each has different customs in its worship.

Activities

1. Explain how Jews worship in the home.
2. Explain the importance of the Torah and the role of leaders in Jewish synagogue worship.
3. 'Worship in the home is more important to Jews than worship in the synagogue.' Do you agree? Give reasons for your answer, showing that you have thought about more than one point of view.

Discussion activity

With a partner, in a small group or as a whole class, discuss whether or not you agree with the Jewish idea of having a day of worship and rest with the family. Explain your opinion.

Summary

You should now be able to explain the importance of Shabbat worship, both in the home and in the synagogue, the role of leaders and the use of sacred writings (the Torah).

2.10 Sikh worship

Worship in the home

Sikhs are taught to remember God constantly and meditate on his name. They can worship at any time, but most use set prayers three times every day – before sunrise (Nitnem), evening (Rahiraas) and at night before sleep (Sohilla). They aim to rise early in the morning, bathe, and then spend time meditating on God. They regard prayer in the home as an important way of discovering God within the soul. This is called Nam simran (calling God to mind). Sikhs believe that the more an individual thinks about God, the more they are filled by God's presence. The idea is to become God-centred rather than self-centred. If the family has a copy of the Sikh scripture, the Guru Granth Sahib, then effectively their home becomes a gurdwara. Most have a copy of the **Gutka** and use it for singing hymns. Most teaching from the passages of scripture takes place at home in the evening when families get together.

Worship in the gurdwara

Although Sikhs do not have a set day for public worship (**Diwan**), in Britain, Sunday is the usual day for community worship in the gurdwara. They may also visit on other days as they see congregational worship as important. Services are informal and may last for five hours, but people come and go during that time. The **granthi** looks after the Guru Granth Sahib in the gurdwara and performs the ceremonial opening of the holy book in the morning and closing in the evening. The book is placed on a raised platform (takht, or throne) under a canopy and covered with a cloth when not being read.

> **Objectives**
> Understand forms of worship in the gurdwara and the home.
> Understand the importance of the Guru Granth Sahib and the Gutka to Sikhs.

> **Key terms**
> **Gutka:** in Sikhism, a collection of daily prayers for Sikhs to use.
> **Diwan:** an act of public worship or service.
> **Granthi:** a reader and explainer of the Guru Granth Sahib and a person who officiates at ceremonies.

A A Sikh gurdwara

During the service, a decorative fan (chauri) is waved over it to symbolically purify the area before the reading of the scripture. The granthi may lead the morning and evening services and read the scriptures, although Sikh public worship can be led by any Sikh, male or female, who is capable of doing so.

On entering the gurdwara, everyone removes their shoes to show respect because they believe that by coming into the presence of the Guru Granth Sahib they come into the presence of God. Everyone bows and kneels in front of the holy book, which is regarded and treated as a living guru. An offering is made of money or food for the gurdwara's kitchen and then the person joins the rest of the **sangat**, the men on one side and the women on the other.

Sacred hymns from the Guru Granth Sahib (kirtan) are sung and there are lectures and sermons explaining them. Musicians lead the singing with the congregation joining in. Prayers are said and readings are made from the Guru Granth Sahib. Near the end of the worship, the Ardas prayer is said. This prayer, which remembers God and the Ten Gurus, includes a request to be faithful to the scriptures and a blessing on the Sikh community and the human race. Specific prayers are said for individuals, for example those who are sick, and karah parshad (food made from flour or semolina, sugar, butter and water) is shared. This is eaten together to show equality and that God blesses all humanity. Following worship, a vegetarian meal is served in the 'free kitchen', the langar.

B *Praying in the gurdwara*

Key terms

Sangat: congregation in a gurdwara.

Discussion activity

With a partner, in a small group or as a whole class, discuss why the Guru Granth Sahib is important for Sikhs. Is there anything more important in their religion? Make notes of the key points to use as examples in the examination.

AQA Examiner's tip

Be aware that Sikhs treat the Guru Granth Sahib as a living guru. They also show it great respect because of its spiritual content.

Activities

1. Explain how Sikhs worship in the home.
2. Explain the role of the granthi and how Sikhs show respect to the Guru Granth Sahib.
3. 'Sikhs show equality in the way they worship.' What do you think? Explain your opinion.

Extension activity

Using the internet or a library, find out more about the function of the langar and its importance to Sikhs. Make notes on the information you discover.

Summary

You should now be able to explain what happens in both private and public worship in Sikhism and the importance of the Guru Granth Sahib and the Gutka.

Assessment guidance

2

Worship – summary

With reference to at least **two** of the religions you have studied, for the examination you should now be able to:

✔ describe and explain ways of worshipping at places of worship and at home, including the key elements of each

✔ explain the use and symbolism of aids to worship, and evaluate their importance

✔ explain the roles of those involved in worship and their importance

✔ understand attitudes to worship in the life of faith

✔ explain the importance of the place of worship (special building)

✔ give details of the day of worship, including its importance and why it was chosen

✔ explain the function and value of worship itself.

Sample answer

1. Write an answer to the following examination question:

   'Worship is a good thing.'

   Do you agree? Give reasons for your answer, showing that you have thought about more than one point of view. Refer to religious arguments in your answer.

   (6 marks)

2. Read the following sample answer:

   > Worship is a waste of time and effort if God does not exist, as no merit will be got from it. Also, it is rather difficult to know if the right God is being worshipped. The Ten Commandments told the Jews that they must worship one particular God and no other because he is a jealous God. What if that God is one of many and is not the most important one? Would worship be a good thing then? Some also say that having to listen to sermons or long talks is not easy and that there are other ways of spending the time.
   >
   > On the other hand, isn't it right to say thank you for the beauty of creation and the provision of all the things that we require to live? If God is the creator, he deserves to be praised and worshipped for giving us life. Worship also helps us to stop and reflect on the valuable things in life and not take them for granted. Also, it gives the opportunity of asking for God's help when we or others need assistance. Sermons during worship help us to understand why we should live moral lives and think of others and not just ourselves. In addition, worship helps people to mix together and share spiritually and socially.
   >
   > So, if God exists, I think worship would be a good thing.

3. With a partner, discuss the sample answer. Do you think that there are other things that the student could have included in the answer?

4. What mark would you give this answer out of 6? (Look at the mark scheme in the Introduction on page 7 (AO2) before you attempt this.) What are the reasons for the mark you have given?

AQA Examination-style questions

1 Look at the photograph and answer the following questions.

(a) Give **two** examples of what a religious leader might do to lead worship. *(2 marks)*

> **AQA Examiner's tip:** A long explanation is not required for each example.

(b) Choose an aid to worship for **each** of the **two** religions you have studied and explain how they might be used. *(4 marks)*

> **AQA Examiner's tip:** If you choose two examples from only one religion, you will only gain a maximum of 2 marks.

(c) 'Singing hymns is the most important part of worship.' What do you think? Explain your opinion. *(3 marks)*

> **AQA Examiner's tip:** Don't forget to compare the importance of singing with other parts of worship, e.g. praying.

(d) Explain briefly the importance of prayer in worship. *(3 marks)*

> **AQA Examiner's tip:** Your answer should be limited to about six lines, as it only has a maximum of 3 marks. You have not been asked to use two religions in your answer, so you don't have to use more than one.

(e) 'All religious believers should worship God every day.'
Do you agree? Give reasons for your answer, showing that you have thought about more than one point of view. Refer to religious arguments in your answer. *(6 marks)*

> **AQA Examiner's tip:** Remember that when you are given a statement and asked 'do you agree?' you must show what you think and the reasons why other people might take a different view. If your answer is one sided, you can only achieve a maximum of 4 marks. If you make no comment about religious belief or practice, you will achieve no more than 3 marks.

3 Pilgrimage

3.1 What is a pilgrimage?

Pilgrimage

A **pilgrimage** is a journey made for religious reasons, often to a shrine or place that is important to someone's faith. A person who goes on such a journey is called a pilgrim. Pilgrims may travel alone or in a group to a special place where they take part in ceremonies and encounter objects and architecture associated with their religion.

'Pilgrim' comes from a Latin word, *peregrinus*, which means someone who is passing through, a traveller or temporary resident. Some people think that this is a good way of describing a person's journey through life on their spiritual path to enlightenment or unity with God. Some people call the inner journey of prayer and meditation that the life of a monk encourages a pilgrimage.

It is clear that there is a strong human instinct to identify certain places as sacred and to link physical and inner journeying. Even in a non-religious culture, wayside shrines of flowers, messages and teddy bears show places where tragedy has occurred. People travel to Graceland, the home of Elvis Presley, or to football grounds, or to places of personal significance to remember or celebrate or to mourn. In this chapter, however, you will be investigating religious places of pilgrimage and their importance for believers.

Special places

People make pilgrimages to special places connected to their religion or beliefs.

- It may be a place linked to their religion's founder or a prophet or leader in the faith, for example their place of birth or death, or where the religion's headquarters are.
- It may be significant in the history of the religion, where something important took place that made a difference to the way the religion developed.
- It may be a place where something extraordinary happened, for example a miracle, which shows how the presence of God can affect human beings.
- It may be a place where the **relics** of a saint or prophet are kept.
- It may be a place with special architecture, for example a church, temple or shrine, or objects like statues, icons or tombs of holy people that inspire awe. The spiritual power of the place is shown in its physical grandeur.

Objectives
Introduce what a pilgrimage is and why people go on a pilgrimage.

Key terms
Pilgrimage: a journey made for religious reasons.

Relic: an object of religious veneration, especially a piece of the body or a personal item of a holy person.

A Some people seek healing on a pilgrimage

Why people make a pilgrimage

- Many pilgrims wish to get close to the origins of their faith and follow in the footsteps of their founder or prophet. This helps believers to visualise where the founder or prophet walked, taught or experienced religious truth, and to experience personally what it must have been like to be there at that time.
- Pilgrimage reminds people of the key events in their faith or focuses on a particular aspect.
- It requires great commitment and sometimes physical hardship.
- It may be a merit-making activity, which brings good kamma (karma) for future rebirth.
- Many pilgrims wish to be forgiven for their sins.
- There may be some hope for a miracle, or for spiritual healing, if they are suffering from illness or hardship.
- For some, it is a religious duty; for others the fulfilment of a vow.
- Many people find pilgrimage a life-changing experience, particularly being part of a large community of believers from their faith.
- Pilgrimage provides an opportunity for believers to refresh their faith. By showing spiritual discipline and expressing their feelings of devotion, they may commit themselves more fully to the teachings and practices of their religion, and this commitment will last long after their pilgrimage ends.

B *A pilgrimage sometimes requires physical hardship*

links

See page 92 for a definition of the terms 'kamma' and 'karma', or you can look them up in the Glossary at the back of this book.

Research activity

1. **a** Using the internet or a library, find out what practical arrangements a person would need to make to go on a pilgrimage to a holy place (or places) in **one** religion you are studying.
   b Design your own package tour, complete with itinerary and advertising poster. Try to include reasons why a religious person might want to go on a pilgrimage to that location.

Activities

1. Explain what is meant by a 'pilgrimage'.
2. Explain how a pilgrimage differs from a holiday.
3. Describe **three** different kinds of places that become places of religious pilgrimage.
4. Explain why people go on a pilgrimage. What do they hope to get out of it?

Discussion activity

With a partner or in a small group, discuss the following statement: 'Places of pilgrimage are there just to make money.' Do you agree? Give reasons for your answer, showing that you have thought about more than one point of view.

AQA Examiner's tip

For each of the two religions you are studying, you need to understand the reasons why some places become special and draw people to them on pilgrimage, and also why people make pilgrimages.

Summary

You should now be able to explain what a pilgrimage is and why people go on a pilgrimage.

3.2 Buddhist holy places

For Buddhists, the purpose of pilgrimage is to turn towards the dharma (teaching), purify one's mind, earn merit, pay tribute to ancient holy sites, seek blessings and be inspired to live a virtuous and positive life.

Four main places linked to events in the Buddha's life became places of pilgrimage. The Buddha was said to have given people permission to visit them.

1. Lumbini, his birthplace
2. Bodh Gaya, where he achieved enlightenment
3. Benares, where he gave his first sermon at Sarnath and gathered disciples
4. Kushinagara, where he died

At all of these places, Buddhists spend some time there in meditation, **prostrate** themselves, make offerings, take part in acts of worship and consult with the monks.

Objectives

Learn about places of pilgrimage linked to the Buddha.

Understand why they are important to Buddhists.

links

See pages 74–75 to find more about the life of the Buddha.

Key terms

Prostrate: lie on the ground face down to show reverence and humility.

Lumbini

Lumbini is in the foothills of the Himalayas, in the district of Nepal. Siddattha Gotama, the Buddha, was born here in around 563 BCE. He was the son of King Shuddhodana and Queen Mahamaya. There is a Holy Pond where Siddattha and his mother bathed, and the remains of their palace. The Mayadevi Temple has been built on the spot where Siddattha was born. From early morning to early evening, pilgrims from different countries perform chanting and meditation there.

A *Prayer flags help Buddhists meditate at Lumbini*

B *The Mahabodhi Temple at Bodh Gaya*

Bodh Gaya

According to tradition, the Buddha sat meditating under a tree near the city of Gaya. It was there that he attained enlightenment and insight into the answers to his search for spiritual truth. From then on, Siddattha was called the Buddha (the Enlightened or Awakened One). The tree under which he sat is known as the Bodhi (enlightenment) Tree, and the place became known as Bodh Gaya. It became a well-known place of pilgrimage for Buddhists.

Emperor Asoka visited Bodh Gaya about 250 years later and built the Mahabodhi Temple there, which was abandoned for centuries. This was restored in the late-19th century and is now the main monastery there.

Benares

Benares, also known as Varanasi (see page 60), is on the west bank of the river Ganges. It is one of the oldest cities in the world and considered holy by both Buddhists and Hindus.

After his enlightenment, the Buddha went to Benares, to the deer park at Sarnath, where he gave his first sermon about the basic teachings of Buddhism. This is also where the Buddha brought the sangha (community) together. The Chaukhandi stupa marks the spot where Buddha met his first disciples again. The Buddha preached many sermons here, which were later written down in the scriptures.

Kushinagara

The Buddha died at Kushinagara at the age of 80. He preached his final sermon and achieved his final enlightenment here. After his death, his body was carried through the city to a shrine where it was cremated.

Today, the Mahaparinirvana Stupa marks the place of the Buddha's death. Nearby is a 1500-year-old image of the Buddha as he attained his final enlightenment. Not far away is the place of his cremation. Pilgrims visit both places, and meditate on the life and death of the Buddha.

Activities

1. Explain the purpose of pilgrimage to a Buddhist.
2. Why do you think no shops and restaurants are allowed near the holy site in Lumbini?
3. How does visiting and meditating at a holy site help a Buddhist in their daily life?

links

Look back to page 12 to remind yourself of what a stupa is.

Research activity

Using the internet or a library, find an account by a Buddhist who has visited one of the sites mentioned. What impact did it have on them?

AQA Examiner's tip

Make sure that you know why each place has become a place of pilgrimage for Buddhists.

Discussion activity

1. With a partner, in a small group or as a whole class:

   a. Discuss which Buddhist site you think is the most important.

   b. Discuss the following statement: 'Pilgrimage is the only way a Buddhist can understand the teachings of the Buddha.'

   Do you agree? Give reasons for your answer, showing that you have thought about more than one point of view.

Summary

You should now be able to describe four sites of pilgrimage for Buddhists, explain what believers do there and why the places are important to them.

3.3 Christian holy places (1)

The importance of pilgrimage

Christians make pilgrimages to:

- be cured of an illness
- express sorrow for sin and receive forgiveness
- experience a holy place
- meet others who share their faith
- help sick or disabled pilgrims.

The journey itself, and the experience of sharing it, bring Christians closer to God and help them learn more about their faith. Many bring back religious mementoes to help them recall the experience to strengthen their spiritual lives. While there, they will pray, take part in acts of worship or re-enactments of the life of Jesus or a saint, or consult with priests or monks. Many will make donations to symbolise the offering of oneself to God.

Bethlehem

Christians consider all of Israel to be the **Holy Land**, but particularly Bethlehem and Jerusalem.

According to scripture, Jesus was born in Bethlehem, the city of David, a famous king of Israel. Joseph and Mary travelled there from Nazareth to register for a census. While there, Mary gave birth to Jesus and placed him in a manger because there was no room in the inn (Luke 2:4–7). After some wise men visited, the family fled to Egypt to escape King Herod's massacre of babies under the age of two (Matthew 2).

Christians visit the 4th-century Church of the Nativity, built on the traditional site of Jesus' birth. In the Grotto beneath the church, pilgrims kiss the silver star on the floor that marks the place of the manger. It is surrounded by 15 lamps representing different Christian communities. A Latin inscription says, 'Here Jesus Christ was born to the Virgin Mary.' Christians pray, meditate and attend services here.

Next door is St Catherine's Roman Catholic Church, which has an altar dedicated to the Holy Innocents, the children whom Herod killed. Archaeologists have found babies' bones that date from the period when Herod carried out his massacre. Midnight Mass is held in this church at Christmas.

> **Objectives**
> Learn about Christian places of pilgrimage, particularly in the Holy Land.
>
> Understand why they are important to Christians.

> **Key terms**
> **Holy Land:** a name given by Christians to Israel.

A *A silver star marks the traditional site of Jesus' birth*

Jerusalem

Jerusalem is a holy city for Christians, Jews and Muslims. Christian pilgrims visit Jerusalem because it is where Jesus ended his ministry. His last supper, passion, death, resurrection and ascension all took place in Jerusalem (Matthew 26 and 27).

Christians visit places connected with the life and death of Jesus to relive his passion. They visit an upper room like the one where the Last Supper was held. In the Garden of Gethsemane they imagine Jesus' suffering before his arrest. They follow the Via Dolorosa (Way of Sorrow) along which Jesus carried his cross to Calvary (Golgotha) and pray with other believers along the way.

B Burial place of Jesus in the Church of the Holy Sepulchre

The Church of the Holy Sepulchre, built in 335 CE to mark the site of the resurrection, is an important shrine. There is also a garden tomb, very like the one described in the Gospels, which evokes the atmosphere of the resurrection in a way the Church of the Holy Sepulchre cannot. Pilgrims may visit the Mount of Olives where Jesus was arrested and was said to have ascended into heaven. At each of these places, pilgrims worship together or meditate alone on the life and death of Jesus.

Activities

1. Explain **three** reasons why Christians might go on a pilgrimage.
2. How might sharing an experience with others strengthen a Christian's faith?
3. Why do you think Christians call Israel the 'Holy Land'?
4. Explain what Christians do at Bethlehem and at Jerusalem to show devotion to Jesus.

Discussion activities

1. Some people dispute whether some of the holy sites in Bethlehem and Jerusalem are historically accurate. Do you think this matters? Explain your opinion.
2. With a partner, in a small group or as a whole class, discuss the following statement: 'Pilgrimage to Jerusalem is the most important thing a Christian can do.' Do you agree? Give reasons for your answer, showing that you have thought about more than one point of view.

Research activity

Using the internet or a library, look up the references to sacred texts mentioned on these pages and record a summary of them for use in your examination.

AQA Examiner's tip

Make sure that you know why each place has become a place of pilgrimage for Christians.

Summary

You should now be able to describe two Christian sites of pilgrimage in the Holy Land, explain what believers do there and why the places are important to them.

3.4 Christian holy places (2)

Rome

Rome is important in the history of the Christian Church:

- St Peter and St Paul were martyred here.
- It contains catacombs where early Christians were buried.
- It contains St Peter's Basilica and the Vatican, the home of the Pope, the head of the Roman Catholic Church.

In the 1st century CE, St Peter and St Paul were martyred and buried in public cemeteries; St Peter on Vatican Hill and St Paul near the Via Ostiense.

Later, wealthy Christians bought land to bury their families in catacombs. The early Christians gathered there to honour their dead. After the great persecutions, they became centres of pilgrimage. Christians from all parts of the Holy Roman Empire visited the catacombs to honour the martyrs and saints of the church, just like pilgrims today.

Especially at Easter, Roman Catholic Christians flock to St Peter's where they hope to hear the Pope speak and receive his blessing in St Peter's Square. They may pray or attend Mass in St Peter's Basilica where St Peter is buried. Other Popes are buried there, so for Catholics it represents an important part of their Church's history. The magnificence of St Peter's inspires pilgrims with awe, and the Pope's words and blessing strengthen their faith and commitment.

> **Objectives**
> Learn about Christian places of pilgrimage, particularly Rome and Lourdes.
>
> Understand why they are important to Christians.

> **links**
> See page 56 to review the importance of pilgrimage for Christians.

Case study: Ancient Christian symbols

The walls of the catacombs contain Christian symbols and pictures that sum up the Christian faith. The Good Shepherd with a lamb around his shoulders represents Christ saving a soul. The 'chi rho' formed by interlacing the first two Greek letters in the word Christos (Christ) means a Christian is buried in that tomb. The fish, a symbol of Christ, is also found there. The Greek word for fish is ichthus. Each Greek letter in the word forms an acrostic: Jesus Christos, Theou Uios Soter which means 'Jesus Christ, Son of God, Saviour'.

A The chi rho symbol

B The Pope speaks to pilgrims in St Peter's Square

> **Activity**
> 1. Read the case study. Why do you think the early Christians used symbols and pictures rather than words?

Lourdes

In 1858, a girl called Bernadette had visions of the Virgin Mary in a cave by the river here. Bernadette described praying the Rosary with Mary who smiled at her with motherly love.

Over time, people have claimed to have been healed at Lourdes. A paralysed woman who recovered the use of her limbs was the first miracle reported. There have been 67 miracles in the last 141 years, and about 6000 other claimed cures. Over 7 million pilgrims visit each year.

Many pilgrims who go to Lourdes are seriously ill or severely handicapped. Young people accompany them as carers. Pilgrims bathe in the water, praying for healing, and light candles at the grotto where the Virgin Mary appeared. Many take part in the Stations of the Cross (life-sized statues representing the suffering and death of Jesus), take part in liturgies and receive the sacraments of Reconciliation and the Eucharist. In a candlelit procession where people of all nationalities pray the Rosary together, hymns are sung in Latin, the church's universal language, representing the unity of all Christians everywhere. Pilgrims often bring home Lourdes water, Rosary beads and other religious articles.

links

Look back to page 36 for information about the Rosary.

C The Basilica of the Immaculate Conception, Lourdes

Activities

2. Explain why Rome is a centre of pilgrimage for Christians.
3. Why do you think it is important for Christians to honour martyrs?

Discussion activity

1. With a partner, in a small group or as a whole class, discuss the following statements:
   a. 'It is wrong to have beautiful buildings like St Peter's Basilica when so many people are poor.'
   b. 'Places like Lourdes hold out false hopes to sick people.'

   Do you agree? Give reasons for your answers, showing that you have thought about more than one point of view.

Research activity

Using the internet or a library, find out more about the young girl who had visions of the Virgin Mary. She was not believed at first, but over time people accepted she was telling the truth. Why do you think the Roman Catholic Church was so reluctant to believe what she said?

AQA Examiner's tip

Make sure that you know why each place has become a place of pilgrimage for Christians.

Summary

You should now be able to describe two Christian sites of pilgrimage, Rome and Lourdes, explain what believers do there and why the places are important to them.

3.5 Hindu holy places

For Hindus, making a pilgrimage is an important way of showing devotion to God, bringing great blessings to those who make the journey in the right spirit. Pilgrims may join a procession, perform acts of worship, consult with priests, read the scripture and give offerings of flowers or food at a holy place.

Many Hindu holy places are connected with water as Hindus believe it comes from, and is part of, God. Bathing symbolises the purity of heart a Hindu must have to appear before God.

The river Ganges

The Ganges is more than a river; she is a goddess, a mother who brings life to the land and people of India. The goddess Ganga came down to earth through the god Shiva's matted hair and formed the river to cleanse the whole earth of sin.

Varanasi

Varanasi (Benares) on the Ganges is said to be the home of Shiva. Hindus believe that bathing in the Ganges will wash away their sins and they will be reborn into a better life. Many Hindus hope to die at Varanasi and to have their ashes scattered on the Ganges. They believe they will escape samsara (the cycle of life, death and rebirth) and attain moksha (release). Pilgrims often take a bottle of Ganges water with them when they return home.

Prayag and Kumbh Mela

Once every 12 years, millions of people share in ritual bathing at the **Kumbh Mela** festival at Prayag (now Allahabad), where the Ganges and Yamuna rivers meet. Prayag (place of sacrifice) is where Brahma

> **Objectives**
> Learn about Hindu places of pilgrimage.
>
> Understand why they are important to Hindus.

> **Key terms**
> **Kumbh Mela:** a major festival in Hinduism. 'Kumbh' means pitcher of divine nectar, 'Mela' means festival.

A *The Kumbh Mela festival*

offered his first sacrifice after creating the world. Hindu legend says gods and demons fought over a pitcher of divine nectar. Drops of nectar fell on Prayag during the battle.

Hindus from all walks of life bathe in the river to be cleansed of their sins. Holy men and women attend, dressed in saffron sheets with ashes and powder dabbed on their skin. After bathing, people are spiritually cleansed and God's blessings are sought. Believers take part in religious discussions, sing hymns and prepare food for the holy men and women and the poor.

Mathura

Pilgrims visit Mathura because **Krishna** was born there when his parents were imprisoned by an evil king. Krishna was his mother's eighth child who was destined to kill the king. Fearing this, the king killed every child, but Krishna's father took him across the river Yamuna to foster parents. Later, the evil king invited Krishna back to Mathura so he could kill him. Instead, Krishna killed the evil king and placed a good king on the throne.

Mathura's main temple is the Keshava Deo Mandir, where Krishna and Radha, the goddess associated with him, are worshipped. There are many holy sites and 12 sacred forests nearby. Vrindavan, the village where Krishna lived, has around 5000 temples. Many elderly worshippers of Vishnu retire here hoping to return at death to the spiritual Vrindavan, where they can spend eternity with Lord Krishna.

> **Key terms**
>
> **Krishna:** an incarnation of the Hindu god Vishnu.

Activities

1. Explain why Hindus value pilgrimage.
2. Explain the significance of water for Hindus.
3. Why do many Hindus wish to die at Varanasi?
4. How might a visit to Mathura help Hindus in their daily lives?

Discussion activity

1. With a partner, in a small group or as a whole class:
   a. Make a list of the benefits of the Kumbh Mela festival for Hindus. Discuss whether there are any disadvantages to worshipping in this way.
   b. Discuss the following statement: 'True pilgrimage is the inner journey of the soul.' What do you think? Explain your opinion.

> **AQA Examiner's tip**
>
> Make sure that you know why each place has become a place of pilgrimage for Hindus.

Summary

You should now be able to describe four sites of pilgrimage for Hindus, explain what believers do there and why the places are important to them.

3.6 Muslim holy places

Makkah

Makkah in Saudi Arabia is Muhammad's birthplace. Muslims have a religious duty to go on **Hajj** at least once in their lifetime, if money and health allow.

Once a year, in the month of Dhul Hijjah, Muslims of every colour, class and ethnic group stand before the **Ka'aba** (a shrine built by Prophet Ibrahim) in the centre of the Grand Mosque. They wear simple white garments that represent the purity of heart (ihram) needed to worship Allah, and show that all Muslims are equal in his sight.

During Hajj, pilgrims perform certain acts of worship:

- They circle the Ka'aba seven times, repeating prayers, some people touching the black stone.
- They walk or run between the hills of Safa and Marwa seven times.
- They sip water from a sacred well (Zam Zam) that appeared in the desert to save Hagar and Ishmael from dying of thirst. Many bring water from the Zam Zam well home with them.
- They stand in the open in the valley of Arafat until sunset praising Allah. The Arabian heat at midday hints at what Judgement Day will be like.
- They climb Mount Arafat, the Mount of Mercy, to confess their sins, listen to a sermon and join in prayers.
- At Mina, they throw pebbles at three stone pillars representing the devil to show they reject evil.
- A sheep or goat is sacrificed, meat given to the poor, and the feast of Eid ul Adha ends Hajj. Muslims celebrate this throughout the world.
- Men shave their heads and women cut a piece of their hair.
- They stone the pillars in Mina again and make a final visit to the Ka'aba before returning home.

The religious meaning of Hajj

Hajj shows obedience and faith in Allah and the unity and equality of all Muslims. During Hajj, the Muslim must observe all the rules and rituals in obedience to Allah's will. It strengthens a Muslim's faith and sense of identity with the worldwide community (ummah). It is a focus for the whole of a Muslim's life and belief.

Madinah

Muhammad spent his later years in Madinah, where he built a mosque and established the ummah. He died and was buried there.

Many pilgrims choose to visit the Prophet's Mosque and grave in Madinah after Hajj. They dress in their best clothes, bringing greetings as though Muhammad were alive. They reflect on Muhammad's life, teachings and his physical presence in the mosque.

Objectives

Learn about Muslim places of pilgrimage.

Understand why they are important to Muslims.

Key terms

Hajj: the annual pilgrimage to Makkah, one of the Five Pillars of Islam.

Ka'aba: the black covered cube-shaped building in the centre of the Grand Mosque in Makkah.

A *The Ka'aba in Makkah*

links

See page 113 to find out more about the festival of Eid ul Adha.

B *The Dome of the Rock, Jerusalem*

Jerusalem

Jerusalem is a holy city for Muslims. In the 7th century CE the Dome of the Rock was built on the site of the second Jewish temple. The mosque contains a rock from where Muhammad ascended to heaven accompanied by the angel Jibril. Nearby is the Al-Aqsa (the farthest) Mosque, named after a chapter in the Qur'an in which Muhammad was transported to Jerusalem during his Night Journey to heaven. Muslims hold these places in high esteem after Makkah and Madinah.

Activities

1. Explain why Makkah is the holiest city for Muslims.
2. Describe the elements of Hajj that show the Muslim belief in equality of all people before Allah.
3. Explain the importance of Madinah and Jerusalem for Muslims.
4. How does Hajj strengthen the life and faith of a Muslim?

Discussion activity

With a partner, in a small group or as a whole class, discuss the following statement: 'Hajj is just an exciting holiday to a warm country.' What do you think? Explain your opinion.

Summary

You should now be able to describe three sites of pilgrimage for Muslims, explain what believers do there and why the places are important to them.

AQA Examiner's tip

Make sure that you know why each place has become a place of pilgrimage for Muslims.

3.7 Jewish holy places

Jerusalem

For Jews, Jerusalem is their Holy City, the biblical Zion and site of King Solomon's Temple. In the Tenakh, pilgrimage to Jerusalem was required of all men three times a year, at Passover, Shavuot and Sukkot (Exodus 23:17). Each festival remembers part of the Exodus: escaping from Egypt; receiving the Ten Commandments; and wandering in the wilderness. Pilgrimages re-enact the salvation history of the Jews physically and spiritually, and allow people to reconfirm their special relationship with God.

King Solomon built the Temple in the 10th century BCE. Inside was the Holy of Holies, which contained the Ark of the Covenant that held the Ten Commandments. The Babylonians destroyed it when they took the Jews captive in the 6th century BCE. After the exile, a second Temple was built that became a place of pilgrimage for Jews from all over the world who came to offer sacrifices, usually during festivals like Passover. During the 1st century BCE, Herod the Great enlarged the Temple, but this second Temple was destroyed in 70 CE by the Romans. All that remains is the **Western Wall**.

> **Objectives**
> Learn about Jewish places of pilgrimage.
> Understand why they are important to Jews.

> **Key terms**
> **Western Wall:** the only remaining part of the second Temple in Jerusalem.

A People praying at the Western Wall

The Western Wall

The Western Wall of the Jerusalem Temple is the most significant place of pilgrimage for Jews, even though there is no longer anywhere to offer sacrifice and the Holy of Holies has been destroyed. Some people are overcome with grief as they stand before the last relic of the holiest place in Judaism. Some will press their lips to the stones as they offer their prayers or push small scraps of paper containing their prayers into the cracks in the wall. The Ark, the cupboard in which the Torah scrolls are kept, is set in the wall nearest to the Temple.

Many young boys become Bar Mitzvah here. They carry the scrolls, read a passage from the Torah, and catch sweets thrown by the women onlookers. It is a great privilege to have this ceremony performed in Jerusalem.

Yad Vashem

Yad Vashem is another place of pilgrimage in Jerusalem. The name was inspired by the words from Isaiah:

> **"** to them I will give within my temple and its walls a memorial and a name… **"**
>
> *Isaiah 56:5*

Yad Vashem on the Mount of Remembrance is a vast complex of museums, monuments and centres for research and teaching resources about the Holocaust. Israel established it in 1953 to remember the lives and personal stories of every one of the 6 million Jews who died.

Some Jews go there to remind themselves of the suffering of their people; others go to remember a family member who died. All who visit do so out of respect for those who died for their faith, to keep the memory of such an atrocity alive, and to pray for peace.

Perhaps the most moving experience for visitors is that of standing in the bare room, lit only by a single flickering candle, and reading the names, embedded in the floor, of the concentration camps in which so many Jews died.

Activities

1. Explain why the city of Jerusalem is so important to Jews.
2. Explain what Jewish people do when they visit the Western Wall.
3. Describe the purpose of Yad Vashem.

Key terms

Yad Vashem: 'a memorial and a name', the Holocaust memorial complex in Jerusalem.

B *The Hall of Names at Yad Vashem remembers 6 million Holocaust victims*

Research activity

Using the internet or a library, find out more about the Temple built by King Solomon over 3000 years ago and its replacement that was extended by Herod the Great. Try to find pictures that reconstruct what it would have been like. This will help you to understand why Jews mourn its destruction.

Discussion activity

1. With a partner, in a small group or as a whole class, discuss the following statements:
   a. 'Jerusalem is a sad place to visit for Jews.'
   b. 'Remembering the Holocaust is no longer relevant today.'

   Do you agree? Give reasons for your answers, showing that you have thought about more than one point of view.

AQA Examiner's tip

Make sure that you know why each place has become a place of pilgrimage for Jews.

Summary

You should now be able to describe Jewish sites of pilgrimage in Jerusalem, explain what believers do there and why the places are important to them.

3.8 Sikh holy places

Pilgrimage is not particularly encouraged in Sikhism. Guru Nanak was asked whether someone should bathe at pilgrimage places. He replied that real pilgrimage is the inner spiritual journey where a person contemplates God's word and develops inner knowledge.

However, **Amritsar** in the Punjab with its **Golden Temple** has become the centre of the Sikh faith and a place of pilgrimage. While there, pilgrims may pray, read or hear the Guru Granth Sahib being read, eat in the langar, bathe in the pool and consult the granthis about spiritual matters.

Amritsar

The fourth Guru, Guru Ram Das, obtained land for a centre of worship in 1577. The fifth Guru, Guru Arjan, built a temple that Sikhs call 'the Lord's house' (Harimandir). The temple was later covered with gold leaf, so it became known as the Golden Temple. It is a source of inspiration for all Sikhs and a living symbol of their religious history.

The temple is set in the centre of the Pool of Nectar with only one path leading to it. Everyone must use the same approach. There are four entrances, one on each side, showing that people from all castes and creeds are welcome. Each doorway requires even important visitors to humble themselves by stepping downwards before entering. The building is rectangular like Hindu temples but with the dome and minarets of Muslim mosques, showing the Sikh desire for unity. Pilgrims usually bathe in the pool before entering. Each morning, heralded by trumpets, the Sikh scripture, the Guru Granth Sahib, is carried from the Akal Takht (see opposite). Pilgrims follow and walk around the Guru Granth Sahib to show respect. Hymns are sung continuously in its presence.

Objectives
Learn about Sikh places of pilgrimage.

Understand why they are important to Sikhs.

Key terms
Amritsar: city in the Punjab which is the centre of Sikh faith. The name means 'pool of nectar'.

Golden Temple: Harimandir or 'the Lord's house' that has become a centre of pilgrimage for Sikhs.

links
See the pictures of the Golden Temple on pages 9 and 22.

A *A pilgrim bathes in the Pool of Nectar*

The Golden Temple was damaged by conflict between Sikh nationalists and the Indian Army who stormed the temple in 1984.

The Five Takhts

The **Five Takhts** (Royal Thrones) are five gurdwaras that have special significance for Sikhs. They are ruling centres for the Khalsa (Sikh community) where many important decisions concerning their religious and social life are made.

1. **Akal Takht** (Eternal Throne) is opposite the Golden Temple. It is the chief centre of religious authority. Sikhs worldwide have to accept decisions taken here about Sikh belief or practice.
2. **Takht Keshgar Sahib** at Anandpur was the birthplace of the Khalsa founded by Guru Gobind Singh in 1699. The Khanda (double-edged sword), used by Guru Gobind Singh to prepare the amrit (sweet water) used in the first Khalsa initiation ceremony, is displayed here.
3. **Takht Patna Sahib** marks the birthplace of Guru Gobind Singh in 1666 and the place where he spent his early years before moving to Anandpur. Guru Nanak and Guru Tegh Bahadur also visited here.
4. **Takht Damdama Sahib** is found at Batinda where Guru Gobind Singh in 1705 prepared the full version of the Guru Granth Sahib.
5. **Takht Sachkhand** in Hazur Sahib is where Guru Gobind Singh died in 1708. It holds his tent where he was convalescing after he was attacked by assassins and where he died.

Key terms

Five Takhts: five gurdwaras or 'royal thrones' considered to be the seat of Sikh authority where decisions are made.

Research activity

Using the internet or a library, find out more about the incidents and events in the life of the Gurus that made these places important to Sikhs.

Activities

1. Explain why the Sikh religion does not place great importance on pilgrimage.
2. Describe **four** features of the Golden Temple that symbolise the equality of all people before God.
3. Explain why the Five Takhts are important to Sikhs.
4. How might visiting the Takhts connected with the life of Guru Gobind Singh strengthen a Sikh's faith?

Extension activity

Find out more about the incident in June 1984 between Sikh nationalists and the Indian army that led to the Golden Temple and Akal Takht being damaged. Should places of worship be involved in political arguments? Explain your opinion.

AQA Examiner's tip

Make sure that you know why each place has become a place of pilgrimage for Sikhs.

Discussion activity

With a partner, in a small group or as a whole class, discuss the following statement: 'It is wrong to spend money on temples.' What do you think? Explain your opinion.

Summary

You should now be able to describe the Golden Temple, explain what believers do there and explain its importance to Sikhs. You should also be able to explain why the Five Takhts are places of Sikh pilgrimage.

3.9 How pilgrimage can change a life

The impact of pilgrimage

A pilgrimage can be a life-changing experience for people. It is a journey of self-discovery in which people have time, away from their 'ordinary' lives, to reflect on what is important in life and what direction they want their life to take. For some people, whose busy lives do not allow much time for silent reflection, the experience of prayerful silence or meditation at a holy site can overwhelm them with love and peace.

Many pilgrimages require a sacrifice. It may just be money to pay for the journey, or giving up home comforts like television for a while. Some pilgrimages involve physical hardship or discomfort, like standing praying all afternoon at Arafat, or bathing in the cold river Ganges during winter. The element of sacrifice helps people to feel humble in the presence of the divine and re-order their priorities in life. It helps people to feel sorrow for sin, a willingness to change and the joy of forgiveness.

Sharing the experience with others has a significant impact. Many people speak of their amazement at the numbers of believers and their great devotion. It is humbling to hear the stories of courageous people who are seeking God's help for difficulties in their lives that are far worse than anything we have experienced. Some pilgrims keep a journal to record the impact of their journey for later reading and remembering, so that its emotional impact is not lost.

> **Objectives**
> Explore the impact and value of a pilgrimage on an individual.

> **AQA Examiner's tip**
> The examination requires knowledge and understanding of the **impact** and **value** of a pilgrimage on a religion and an individual.
> Its **impact** means how it affects someone or the religion itself.
> Its **value** means what someone gets out of going on a pilgrimage, or how the religion benefits from the practice of pilgrimage.
> These two ideas are not entirely separate. The impact affects the value. A pilgrimage is only valuable if the impact it makes is positive.

The impact may not always be positive. Huge crowds, commercialism, or inaccurate claims about the historical significance of some places may put some people off. Many of the sites attract tourists who do not regard the place as holy and create a distraction for those seeking spiritual strength.

The value of pilgrimage

For people whose pilgrimage has made a positive impact on their life and beliefs, its value is tremendous. They are refreshed spiritually (and possibly physically) and can resume their lives with a new attitude. They may have

A *Praying with other pilgrims can strengthen faith*

learned things they did not know about their religion, or have come to a greater understanding of their beliefs. They have received the moral support of fellow pilgrims and perhaps made new friends. Their lives are enriched by the experience of helping others, for example elderly or disabled pilgrims or the poor.

Case study

The Hajj documentary on Channel 4

In February 2003, Channel 4 showed a film that followed five quite different people as they performed Hajj. At the end, they described the impact the pilgrimage had on them. They felt they had changed irrevocably in the Saudi desert.

Aamer said he felt closer to Allah and could feel the presence of his father (who had died recently) during Hajj. Serfraz said he found it beautiful and asked, 'Is there any other event in life where everybody from every nation comes together as one? It's like one heartbeat, one pulse and we all pray in the one direction.' Kosser said that throughout her life she had a picture of Makkah and the Ka'aba in her head. Now that she had seen it, she would never be able to forget. 'It is a memory that I will cherish for the rest of my life.' Mohammed thought Hajj was a major boost to faith that could go up and down depending on how much good and evil people were exposed to. Hallalah said her focus was different and she had a clearer vision of what she should be doing in life. 'Hajj is an investment in your soul.' The Channel 4 team said, 'Our pilgrims' lives will never be the same again.'

B *The Hajj at Makkah*

Activity

1. Read the case study. Explain the impact and value of Hajj for those individuals.

Activities

2. How does pilgrimage encourage self-discovery?
3. Explain the sacrifices someone might have to make when going on a pilgrimage.
4. Explain how sharing the experience with others helps some people.
5. Explain why some people may not find pilgrimage as uplifting as others.

Discussion activity

1. With a partner, in a small group or as a whole class, discuss the following statements:
   a. 'It is better to go on a pilgrimage alone than with others.'
   b. 'The impact of a pilgrimage does not last.'

   Do you agree? Give reasons for your answers, showing that you have thought about more than one point of view.

AQA Examiner's tip

Apply the general principles outlined on these two pages to the particular pilgrimages in the religions you have studied.

Summary

You should now be able to explain the impact a pilgrimage may have on an individual and how this is valuable to them.

3.10 The importance of pilgrimage to a religion

The impact of pilgrimage on a religion

Most religions encourage their followers to go on a pilgrimage. They are aware of its positive impact on both the individual and the religion.

- Pilgrimage brings the community of believers together, united in one common goal.
- It preserves the traditions of the religion through customs and practices, and by keeping alive the stories associated with the faith.
- It may attract non-believers or people of other faiths who look in admiration at the vast numbers or piety of the pilgrims and seek more information about the faith or ask to join.
- It may draw people who no longer practise the religion back to a religious way of life.
- It may attract media attention and raise the profile of the religion, or correct poor impressions of a faith by seeing what people really do. This was the stated goal of the people who took part in the television programme on Hajj.

Pilgrimage also has a practical impact on a religion. The religious community that owns the holy sites may need assistance in preserving them. Most holy places require the kind of facilities for pilgrims that holiday destinations need for tourists, for example food and accommodation. Health and safety measures must be in place and much organisation is needed to make the pilgrimage experience rewarding for all participants.

Objectives

Explore the impact of pilgrimage on a religion and its value.

AQA Examiner's tip

Sikhism does not place great importance on pilgrimage, although Sikhs do make pilgrimages (see page 66). You need to know generally the impact and value of pilgrimage to a religion, so you may wish to consider it from the perspective of another religion as well.

links

Look back to page 69 to remind yourself about the Channel 4 Hajj documentary.

See page 120 to find out more about the Dalai Lama.

Case study

The value of pilgrimages

In 2007, the Buddhist leader the Dalai Lama wrote about the value of pilgrimages. Pilgrims are profoundly moved by the 'charged' atmosphere of a holy place. They gain merit through hardship and are transformed through the discipline of going barefoot or reciting prayers or mantras. They are filled with the sense of spiritual progress, achieving inner peace and a kind heart.

Moreover, pilgrimages in which people visit other religions' holy places and, if possible, pray together or, if not, meditate silently with each other, are immensely valuable and deep experiences, nurturing understanding and harmony among religions.

The Dalai Lama recalled feeling deep admiration for Christianity when standing before the statue of Mary at Lourdes where millions find peace. In Jerusalem, he prayed with Jewish friends at the Western Wall, with Christians at Christian sites, and with Muslims at the Dome of the Rock.

More recently, he joined Christian and Buddhist leaders in a pilgrimage of prayers, meditation and dialogue at Bodh Gaya. Each morning under the Bodhi Tree, they all sat together and meditated. This was the first meeting of its kind since the two religions began.

A *The Dalai Lama*

Just as for individuals, there may be a negative impact on a religion, too. It might make people less inclined to take the religion seriously if they think they are making money out of a place of spiritual importance.

The value of pilgrimage to a religion

When pilgrimage has a positive impact on believers, its value to a religion is evident. Pilgrimage gives believers a concrete way of expressing their faith. It gives the religion a public identity and shows how its beliefs and teachings are put into practice. It is a way of saying, 'This is what we are about. This is our faith and how we think people should live. These are our values.' It gives a focus for celebrating the religion's way of life. If more people are attracted to the religion, that is good, but it is not the aim of the pilgrimage to gain more followers. Its value is seen in the spiritual and moral lives of believers.

Activities

1. Read the case study. What kind of pilgrimages did the Dalai Lama think were particularly valuable to religions?

2. What do you think might be the impact of the Dalai Lama's visit to Lourdes or to the Christian, Jewish and Muslim sites of pilgrimage in Jerusalem?

Activities

3. Explain how a religion benefits from its followers going on pilgrimage.

4. Describe **three** practical considerations that the religious authorities have to think about at a place of pilgrimage.

5. How does a pilgrimage give a religion a 'public identity'?

Discussion activity

1. With a partner, in a small group or as a whole class, discuss the following statements:
   a. 'Religions should not allow pilgrimages to be filmed.'
   b. 'Visiting pilgrimage sites of other people's religions is a waste of time.'

   Do you agree? Give reasons for your answers, showing that you have thought about more than one point of view.

AQA Examiner's tip

Apply the general principles outlined on these two pages to the particular pilgrimages in the religions you have studied.

Summary

You should now be able to explain the impact a pilgrimage may have on a religion and explain how this is valuable to the religion.

Assessment guidance

3

Pilgrimage – summary

With reference to at least **two** of the religions you have studied, for the examination you should now be able to:

✔ describe the key places of pilgrimage
✔ explain why religious people go on a pilgrimage
✔ describe and explain events linked to pilgrimage
✔ describe and explain people linked to pilgrimage
✔ explain the symbolism involved in pilgrimage
✔ describe and explain practices that take place on a pilgrimage
✔ explain and evaluate the impact of pilgrimage on a religion and on an individual
✔ explain and evaluate the value of pilgrimage to a religion or an individual
✔ consider and discuss attitudes to the place or role of pilgrimage in a modern society.

> **AQA Examiner's tip**
> Remember that you must refer to pilgrimage in two religions in the examination.

Sample answer

1. Write an answer to the following examination question:

    'Pilgrimages are just like holidays.'
    Do you agree? Give reasons for your answer, showing that you have thought about more than one point of view. Refer to religious arguments in your answer.
    (6 marks)

2. Read the following sample answer:

    > I think pilgrimages are just like holidays in the sense that people enjoy going away, they get excited about their trip and want to make it a really special occasion. If people have to leave their country to go on a pilgrimage, they have to make all the same sorts of preparations as if they were going on holiday, so the experience is similar in a way. The big difference is that the person is doing this for a religious reason, to deepen their relationship with God.

3. With a partner, discuss the sample answer. Do you think that there are other things that the student could have included in the answer?

4. What mark would you give this answer out of 6? (Look at the mark scheme in the Introduction on page 7 (AO2) before you attempt this.) What are the reasons for the mark you have given?

AQA Examination-style questions

1. Look at the drawing and then answer the following questions.

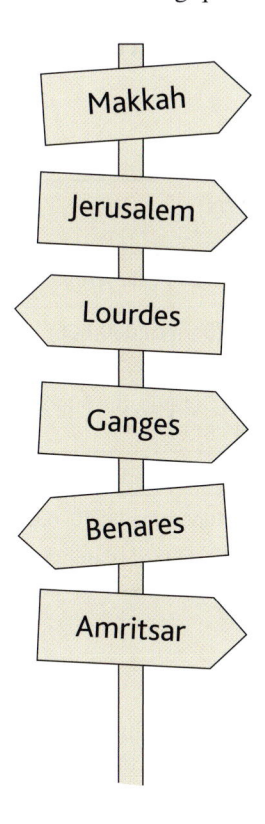

   Signpost showing: Makkah, Jerusalem, Lourdes, Ganges, Benares, Amritsar

   (a) Explain briefly why some places become places of pilgrimage. *(3 marks)*

   (b) Explain what religious believers do as part of a pilgrimage in **each** of **two** religions. *(6 marks)*

   (c) 'Daily prayer is more important than pilgrimage.' What do you think? Explain your opinion. *(3 marks)*

   (d) 'Pilgrimage places too great a burden on a religious believer.' Do you agree? Give reasons for your answer, showing that you have thought about more than one point of view. Refer to religious arguments in your answer. *(6 marks)*

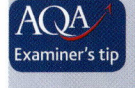

   > **AQA Examiner's tip:** Remember that when you are given a statement and asked 'do you agree?' you must show what you think and the reasons why other people might take a different view. If your answer is one sided, you can only achieve a maximum of 4 marks. If you make no comment about religious belief or practice, you will achieve no more than 3 marks.

4 Origins and beliefs

4.1 Beginnings: Hinduism, Buddhism and Sikhism

A Timeline of major religions and their founders

Approximate date of origin	Religion	Founder(s)
pre-2000 BCE	Hinduism	Origins in Indus Valley/Aryan culture
2000+ BCE	Judaism	Abraham (born c.2000 BCE) Moses (1500–1350 BCE)
c.483 BCE	Buddhism	Siddattha Gotama, the Buddha (563–483 BCE)
30 CE	Christianity	Jesus Christ (1–33 CE)
600 CE	Islam	Prophet Muhammad (570–632 CE)
1500 CE	Sikhism	Guru Nanak (1469–1538 CE)

CE   Common Era (starting 1 AD)
BCE Before Common Era

Hinduism is the oldest religion, over 4500 years old. Buddhism and Sikhism emerged from Hinduism, as both the Buddha and Guru Nanak were Hindus.

Hinduism

Hinduism is a complex religion that has developed over centuries. Its origins are unclear, but it has been traced back to the Indus Valley and to Aryan culture that had many gods.

Today, there are many different Hindu groups. Some worship the same gods but not all share the same beliefs. Hinduism is more like a family of religions with no single scripture, no set pattern of worship, and no clear institutional structure. Hindus call their faith 'the eternal way of conduct', divine in origin and covering every aspect of life.

Hinduism does not have an historical founder, but some holy men have influenced their religion, for example Adi Shankara or Dayananda Saraswati.

Buddhism

Siddattha Gotama was a Hindu prince who grew up surrounded by luxury, shielded from knowledge of suffering. At 19, he married Yasodhara and had a son, Rahula. On his trips outside the palace Siddattha saw the 'four sights' that shocked him. He saw people suffering from old age, sickness and death. He also saw a holy man with no possessions who was living a spiritual life.

Objectives

Introduce the origins of Hinduism, Buddhism and Sikhism and the lives of their founders (if applicable).

links

Look back to Chapter 3 to remind yourself about the many founders or prophets connected with places of pilgrimage.

Research activity

Using the internet or a library, find out more details about the origins of one religion and the places described in its history. If you are studying Hinduism, find out more about the holy men mentioned here and how they influenced Hindu thinking.

B A statue representing the Buddha

Siddattha realised wealth would not protect him from suffering and death. When he was 29, he shaved his head and left his family to live as a holy man. This is called 'the great renunciation'. For six years, he lived a life of strict discipline. He trained himself to eat so little that he nearly starved. He realised this only created more suffering, so he ate some food and sat down under a tree to meditate.

Siddattha wanted to find the truth about how to overcome suffering. As he meditated, he battled with temptations but became the Enlightened One or Buddha. He spent his life teaching others the truths he had learned. The **Buddha** is not considered a god, but someone who has attained **nibbana**, the highest spiritual enlightenment.

Sikhism

Sikhism was revealed through Ten Gurus (religious teachers). The first Guru, **Guru Nanak**, was born in 1469 CE into a high caste Hindu family in the Punjab. It was a time of great conflict between Muslims and Hindus. It is said that as a child he showed exceptional skill as a poet and student of Islam and Hinduism.

When he was 30, Guru Nanak had a life-changing religious experience. While bathing in the river Bain with his Muslim friend Mardana, he disappeared and was presumed drowned. Three days later, he appeared at the same spot as if in a trance. He finally spoke and said, 'There is neither Hindu, nor Muslim. So whose path shall I follow? I will follow God.' Sikhs believe he spent three days in God's presence.

Over 30 years, he made spiritual journeys through India, Tibet and Arabia. He spent the end of his life at Kartarpur, where he established the first Sikh community, including the langar (communal kitchen). His teachings and hymns praising God form part of the Adi Granth (first scriptures).

Key terms

Buddha: historically the Buddha – the enlightened one; an awakened or enlightened person.

Nibbana (nirvana): the state of perfect peace which results from ending all greed, hatred and ignorance.

Guru Nanak: the first Guru and founder of the Sikh faith (1469–1539 CE).

Discussion activity

With a partner, in a small group or as a whole class, discuss the following statement: 'It is impossible to overcome suffering.' What do you think? Explain your opinion.

AQA Examiner's tip

Hinduism does not have a founder, but you should be able to describe its origins. You will not be asked directly about its holy men, but you may use them as examples in an answer.

Activities

1. Describe what is known about the origins of Hinduism.
2. Why do you think there are so many different beliefs and customs in Hinduism?
3. Why do you think the four sights had such an impact on Siddattha?
4. Explain how Guru Nanak's upbringing and experiences led him to the view that God loves all people, no matter who they are.

Extension activity

Each of these three religions started in a different way. Consider what in each case led to the start of the religion and how its start influenced the way in which the religion has developed.

Summary

You should now be able to describe the origins of Hinduism, Buddhism and Sikhism, and describe the lives of Siddattha Gotama and Guru Nanak.

4.2 Beginnings: Judaism, Christianity and Islam

Judaism is nearly 4000 years old. Christianity emerged from Judaism as **Jesus** was a Jew. Nearly 600 years later, Islam arrived. **Muhammad** accepted Jewish prophets and Jesus as part of the revelation.

■ Judaism

Judaism's origins can be traced back to **Abraham**, the first man to believe in one God. He showed absolute faith when God called him to leave his home in Ur in Babylonia and go to the land of Canaan (modern Israel). God made a **covenant** with Abraham that he would be the father of a great nation. Despite their advanced age, Abraham and his wife Sarah had a son, Isaac. The covenant passed to Isaac's son Jacob.

Some people say that Judaism started about 600 years later when **Moses** received the Torah (God's teaching) at Mount Sinai, which spelled out the terms of the covenant. Moses had safely led the Jewish slaves from Egypt across the Red Sea to freedom, an event commemorated at Passover. Moses' leadership as a lawgiver in the wilderness helped the Jews to reach the Promised Land.

Abraham and Moses are considered to be the founding fathers of Judaism.

> **Objectives**
> Introduce the origins of Judaism, Christianity and Islam and the lives of their founders or prophets.

> **links**
> Look back to page 74 to see the timeline of religions.
>
> Look back to Chapter 3 to remind yourself about the many founders or prophets connected with places of pilgrimage.

> **Key terms**
> **Jesus Christ:** 1st-century Jewish teacher and holy man, believed by Christians to be the Son of God.
>
> **Muhammad:** the last and greatest of the prophets of Allah; Muhammad means 'praised'.

A *Moses*

B *Jesus and his disciples at the Last Supper*

Christianity

For Christians, Jesus (God saves) is more than a prophet; he is the Son of God. His life is recorded in the Gospels where he is called the Messiah or Christ (the anointed one). He lived in Nazareth with his mother Mary and her husband Joseph, a carpenter.

When Jesus was about 30 he was baptised in the river Jordan and began his public ministry. While fasting in the wilderness he was tempted by the devil but overcame him. He performed many healing miracles, cast out demons and raised the dead. He taught people through parables and gathered disciples.

The Jewish leaders did not believe he was God's son and plotted to kill him. He was betrayed by his disciple, Judas Iscariot, tried and found guilty of blasphemy. After being whipped and crowned with thorns, he was crucified with two criminals. Three days later, Jesus rose from the dead. He appeared to his followers over the next 40 days. He ascended to heaven and promised to return.

Islam

For Muslims, Muhammad is the 'seal of the prophets', the last and greatest prophet. Born in Makkah in 570 CE, Muhammad was six when his parents died. He was brought up by his grandfather and then his uncle, Abu Talib. As a camel driver, Muhammad gained a reputation for honesty. He married his employer, Khadijah, a wealthy widow.

Muhammad often meditated alone in the caves near Makkah. When he was 40, he received a revelation from **Allah** through the angel Jibril (Gabriel) who commanded him to 'Recite!' Muhammad, though terrified, recited words written on his heart. This was known as the Night of Power. Two years later, Jibril commanded him to preach the words of Allah. He became a preacher and prophet, continuing to receive revelations that his friends recorded in the Qur'an.

The people of Makkah rejected his challenge to give up cheating, gambling, drinking, fighting and worshipping idols. Muhammad fled to Madinah in 622 CE, an event known as the Hijrah (departure) that marks the beginning of the ummah (the Muslim worldwide family). In 630 CE, he returned with an army and conquered Makkah in the name of Allah. He returned to Madinah and died there in 632 CE.

Activities

1. Explain why Abraham is considered to be the father of the Jewish people.
2. Why was Moses so important to the development of the Jewish religion?
3. How is the Christian understanding of who Jesus is different from other religions' understanding of their founder or prophet?
4. Explain why Muslims call Muhammad the 'seal of the prophets'.

Summary

You should now be able to describe the origins of Judaism, Christianity and Islam, and describe the lives of their founders and prophets.

Key terms

Abraham: one of the Founding Fathers of Judaism.

Covenant: God's agreement to look after the Jews as his chosen people and, in return, the Jews' agreement to obey God.

Moses: one of the Founding Fathers of Judaism who led the Israelites in the exodus from Egypt and received the Ten Commandments on Mount Sinai

Allah: the Islamic name for God.

Discussion activity

With a partner, in a small group or as a whole class, discuss the following statement: 'Jews, Christians and Muslims have many prophets in common, so they should all join together as one religion.' Do you agree? Give reasons for your answer, showing that you have thought about more than one point of view.

Research activity

Using the internet or a library, find out more details about the founder(s) of one religion and the places described in its history.

links

See page 87 to find out more about the ummah.

Extension activity

For each of two religions, write a paragraph about the importance of their founders or prophets to followers of that religion today.

AQA Examiner's tip

Make sure that you know why founders and prophets of the religions you have studied are so important to believers today.

4.3 Beliefs about God

Buddhism

Buddhists do not believe in a being (God) who controls the universe outside the laws of nature and human actions. They do not worship the Buddha, but some may worship gods because of local customs. Buddhism does not deny these **deities**, but believes they cannot by themselves free people from samsara (the cycle of life, death and rebirth).

Mahayana Buddhists believe that other Buddhas who lived before Siddattha inhabit **Buddha heavens**. The Buddha was said to have visited these heavens. Mahayana shrines often contain images of previous Buddhas and bodhisattvas ('beings of enlightenment') who spend their lives assisting others). Worshippers address these bodhisattvas directly.

Christianity

Many Christians believe in the **Trinity**. God is one, but reveals himself in three persons:

- God the Father – creator and sustainer of the universe
- God the Son – the saviour who became a man and lived among people (the incarnation)
- God the Holy Spirit – comforter and guide, God's living presence in a person's life

Christians see God as all-powerful, all-loving, all-knowing, perfect and eternal (without beginning or end). The Bible also shows God as a mother, fortress, shepherd, judge and king. Jesus described God as forgiving, compassionate, gracious and faithful to his promises.

Hinduism

Most Hindus believe in one unchanging, eternal, Supreme Spirit, **Brahman**, the Ultimate Reality or Being itself. Brahman is expressed through deities that show different aspects of God's character. Three important deities: Brahma (the creator); Vishnu (the preserver); and Shiva (the destroyer) are called the **Trimurti**. There are other popular deities:

- **Krishna:** an incarnation of Vishnu (see page 61)
- **Kali:** wife of Shiva, goddess of destruction
- **Lakshmi:** wife of Vishnu and goddess of fortune and wealth
- **Rama:** hero of the epic poem the 'Ramayana', an incarnation of Vishnu who symbolises righteousness
- **Ganesha:** elephant-headed god of new ventures, remover of obstacles

Objectives

Explore beliefs about God in the six world religions.

Key terms

Deities: gods or images of gods.

Buddha heavens: other worlds populated by Buddhas who lived in previous worlds.

Trinity: the belief that the three persons of Father, Son and Holy Spirit are all distinct, but are also one being.

Brahman: the Ultimate Reality from which everything comes and into which everything will return.

A *Ganesha – a Hindu god*

Activities

1. Explain Buddhist beliefs about God and 'gods'.
2. Why do you think Christians picture God as a shepherd, mother, or king?
3. Explain how different aspects of God's character are shown through Hindu deities.

Islam

Belief in **tawhid**, the oneness of Allah, is at the heart of Islam. To regard anything as Allah's equal is the worst of all sins. No pictures of Allah are allowed as people might worship them as idols.

Allah is creator, sustainer and owner of all things. He is all-knowing, all-powerful, beyond human understanding, the source of all goodness. He is compassionate, merciful, wise, infinite, the one and only true God, master of the Day of Judgement. His nature is impossible to describe, but the Qur'an reveals 99 names or qualities of Allah.

Judaism

Jews believe in one God, creator, sustainer and ruler of the universe. He continues to work in the world affecting everything people do. He revealed his name (Yahweh, 'I am') to Moses, but God is so holy, Jews use 'Lord' (Adonai) in prayer. In conversation, many say **HaShem** instead of 'God' to show their respect.

Many Jews believe that God is merciful, full of compassion, love and faithfulness (Exodus 34:6), but also just. He will bless those who are faithful, but sinners can expect punishment.

Sikhism

Sikh beliefs about God are contained in the opening sentence of the Guru Granth Sahib, called the **Mool Mantar**. This is part of the **Japji**, which Sikhs recite every morning. There is one God (Nam), creator and sustainer of everything, timeless, formless, fearless, without hatred, eternally true. God is unseen, infinite, beyond human comprehension, a pure spirit who is in every human heart. God reveals himself through his creation so can be loved and worshipped as a father, mother, protector and shelter for people.

Key terms

Trimurti: three Hindu gods (Brahma, Vishnu and Shiva) who control three main aspects of existence – creation, preservation and destruction.

Tawhid: in Islam, the belief that God is One without parts or divisions.

HaShem: in Judaism, the word for God used in ordinary conversation. It means 'The Name'.

Mool Mantar: the first section of the Guru Granth Sahib. It describes Waheguru (Sikhism).

Japji: the long hymn which starts the Adi Granth (Sikhism).

B *The Ik Onkar symbol in Sikhism means 'God is One'*

Activities

4. Why do Muslims forbid pictures of Allah?
5. Explain why Jews use the word 'HaShem' when speaking about God.
6. Why do you think Sikhs recite the Japji every morning?

Discussion activity

With a partner, in a small group or as a whole class, discuss the following statement: 'It is impossible to know that God is loving and forgiving.' Do you agree? Give reasons for your answer, showing that you have thought about more than one point of view. Make a note of the key points to use in your examination.

AQA Examiner's tip

Although Hindus have many deities, they are monotheists (they believe in one God, Brahman).

The qualities of God for many faiths are generally the same. This section has emphasised certain ones for each religion, but that does not mean they do not share a belief in the others.

Summary

You should now be able to explain beliefs about God in the two religions you are studying.

4.4 Buddhist beliefs

The Three Marks of Existence

The Buddha taught that there are three universal truths about life (the **Three Marks of Existence**):

1. **Anicca** (everything changes). Nothing in the universe lasts for ever. The landscape, plants, people are changing all the time. Nothing is permanent.
2. **Anatta** (people change). Anatta means 'no permanent identity or soul'. People are made up of consciousness, feelings, thoughts, sight or perception and physical bodies. As we grow from babies to adults, our minds, knowledge, even our personalities, change. Nothing is fixed.
3. **Dukkha** (life is unsatisfactory). People can never be satisfied with life. Everything we know and love changes and will eventually die. Everyone suffers from boredom, sickness, accidents, old age and death. Even if we had everything we desired, we would not be permanently happy.

The Four Noble Truths

The Buddha was like a doctor who sees a patient's symptoms, finds their cause and prescribes a cure. The **Four Noble Truths** describe what is wrong (dukkha), what causes it (tanha), how to cure it (nirodha), and what is the best way of curing it (magga).

1. **Dukkha:** Everyone suffers or finds life unsatisfactory and frustrating at times, as nobody is perfect until they reach enlightenment.
2. **Tanha** (desire or craving): The Buddha thought that people were selfish, greedy and possessive of people and things. People suffer because they are never satisfied with what they have, they always want more. Three 'poisons' of ignorance, greed and hatred cause more suffering.
3. **Nirodha:** The way to overcome suffering is to get rid of craving and desire by discovering inner satisfaction or reaching enlightenment as the Buddha did.
4. **Magga:** The Buddha had lived in luxury and in extreme hardship, but neither helped him overcome suffering. He therefore taught a Middle Way between these two extremes that would help someone overcome dukkha. This is set out in the Noble **Eightfold Path**.

Objectives

Understand key Buddhist beliefs.

Key terms

Three Marks of Existence: the truth about all things. They do not last (anicca), they have no soul that lives on after death (anatta) and they result in suffering (dukkha).

Four Noble Truths: dukkha, tanha, nirodha, magga (suffering, the cause of suffering, the end of suffering, the path to the end of suffering).

Eightfold Path: the way to wisdom; mental training and the way of morality (eight stages to be practised simultaneously).

links

See page 97 for more on the Five Moral Precepts.

See page 75 for a definition of nibbana, or you can look it up in the Glossary at the back of this book.

Activities

1. Even if you won the lottery and had everything you wanted, would you be permanently happy? Explain your opinion.
2. Explain the meaning of each of the Three Marks of Existence.
3. Explain the meaning of the Four Noble Truths.

The Noble Eightfold Path

The way to wisdom

1. **Right viewpoint:** Having the right understanding about life as described in the Four Noble Truths.
2. **Right intention:** Following the path for the right reasons. It is commitment to the spiritual path, the positive thinking that leads to unselfishness and caring for others.

The way of morality

3. **Right speech:** People should be kind, gentle, truthful, helpful and not hurt each other with words.
4. **Right action:** People should follow Five Moral Precepts, undertaking to abstain from harmful or improper actions.
5. **Right living:** People should work to the best of their ability in an occupation that does not involve killing or hurting others.

The way of mental development

6. **Right effort:** People should train their minds to avoid things that are negative and evil and concentrate on good things.
7. **Right mindfulness:** People should develop the ability to control their minds so that they are aware of what is happening around them and in their minds. This is helped by meditation.
8. **Right concentration:** People should train their minds to 'let go' of unwanted thoughts. Through meditation they can become calm and peaceful, and ultimately escape **samsara** and achieve nibbana.

A *The Noble Eightfold Path, shown as a wheel with eight spokes*

Activities

4. Describe **three** examples of jobs that a Buddhist would not take.
5. Explain how meditation can help a Buddhist overcome suffering.

Key terms

Samsara: the circle of birth, death and rebirth, which can be transcended by following the Eightfold Path.

AQA Examiner's tip

You need to consider how these beliefs affect the way Buddhists live their lives.

Research activity

Using the internet or a library, find out more about how Buddhists try to overcome suffering in the world in practical ways. You can find out about the work of a Buddhist charity at www.karuna.org.

Discussion activity

1. With a partner, in a small group or as a whole class, discuss the following statements:
   a. 'Getting rid of craving and desire will not stop people from suffering.'
   b. 'The Five Moral Precepts are too difficult for anyone to follow.'

   Do you agree? Give reasons for your answers, showing that you have thought about more than one point of view.

Summary

You should now be able to explain key Buddhist beliefs.

4.5 Christian beliefs

■ The Apostles' Creed

A creed is a summary of beliefs. **The Apostles' Creed** (4th century CE) was not actually written by the apostles, but is based on their teaching. It describes key beliefs about God's work in the Trinity, the creation, his incarnation as Jesus, the Holy Spirit, salvation and eternal life.

> *I believe in God, the Father almighty, maker of heaven and earth.*

Christians believe that the all-powerful God (the 'Father' in the Trinity) created the universe.

> *I believe in Jesus Christ, his only Son, our Lord. He was conceived by the power of the Holy Spirit and born of the Virgin Mary.*

Jesus, God's only Son, was born from a human mother, Mary, who was still a virgin when she became pregnant. God's Holy Spirit brought this about. Christians believe that Jesus is both human and divine (God made man).

> *He suffered under Pontius Pilate, was crucified, died and was buried. He descended into hell.*

Pontius Pilate, the Roman Governor in Jerusalem, judged Jesus and, despite his innocence, ordered his crucifixion. He was buried in a tomb carved out of a rock with a stone rolled across its entrance. The tomb was guarded by Roman soldiers. Jesus joined those who had already died.

> *On the third day he rose again.*

Early Sunday morning, women found the stone rolled away and the tomb empty. Jesus appeared to his disciples on a number of occasions. They talked and ate with him. The Gospels make it clear that Jesus was truly alive and not a ghost.

> *He ascended into heaven, and is seated at the right hand of God, the Father Almighty.*

Objectives
Understand key Christian beliefs.

Key terms
Apostles' Creed: a statement setting out the beliefs of the Christian faith, based on the central teachings of the apostles.

∞ links
Look back to page 78 to remind yourself of what Christians believe about God, the Trinity and Jesus.

Look back to pages 56–57 to remind yourself of Christian beliefs about the resurrection of the body and life everlasting.

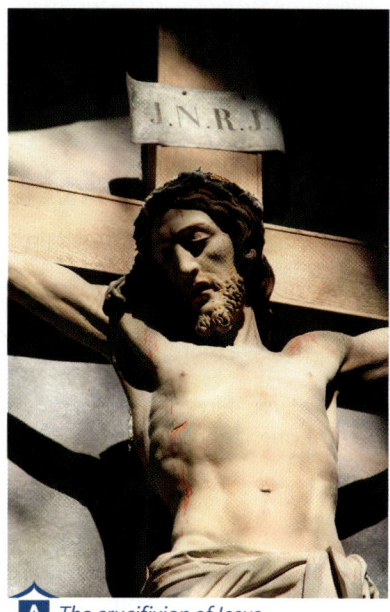

A *The crucifixion of Jesus*

Forty days after the resurrection, Jesus returned to God, and his appearances stopped. Being seated at God's right hand, the place of honour for a guest at a banquet, shows the honour and glory of his divinity and suggests the start of his reign over the Kingdom of God that he preached on earth.

> He will come again to judge the living and the dead.

Jesus will conduct the Last Judgement (see page 92).

> I believe in the Holy Spirit,

Christians believe that God's Holy Spirit, sent to the apostles at Pentecost, is God's presence at work in people's hearts. No one can see God, but Christians say they feel his presence when they pray or act wisely or kindly. They believe the Holy Spirit awakens faith in people and guides the Church in making decisions.

> the holy catholic Church, the communion of saints,

The Church here is not a building but all people who follow Jesus. The word 'catholic' means worldwide, not 'Roman Catholic'. Christians believe the Church is holy and universal. The communion of saints is the fellowship of all Christians, living and dead.

> the forgiveness of sins,

Jesus preached forgiveness, and the risen Jesus gave the disciples the power to free people from their sins. Baptism is a sign of God's great love and forgiveness.

> the resurrection of the body, and the life everlasting. Amen.

As Jesus rose to new life in a glorified body, Christians believe they will also rise to new life, although it is impossible to understand exactly how this will be.

Summary

You should now be able to explain key Christian beliefs.

Activities

1. Explain Christian beliefs about Jesus' birth.
2. Why do you think the day Jesus was crucified is now called 'Good Friday'?
3. Christians believe that Jesus' resurrection proves that there is eternal life. What do you think? Explain your opinion.
4. Explain what the creed means by 'the holy catholic Church, the communion of saints, the forgiveness of sins'.

Discussion activity

With a partner, in a small group or as a whole class, discuss the following statement: 'The body of Jesus must have been stolen.' What do you think? Explain your opinion.

Research activity

Using the internet or a library, find out how the New Testament describes the events of Jesus' death, resurrection and ascension into heaven and the coming of the Holy Spirit to the disciples on Pentecost.

AQA Examiner's tip

You need to consider how these beliefs affect the way Christians live their lives.

4.6 Hindu beliefs

Four aims of life

Hindu scriptures describe four aims of life:

1. **Dharma** (doing one's duty) means fulfilling responsibilities that come with each stage of life and living a moral life. Carrying out religious duties brings good karma.
2. **Artha** means earning an honest living. The goal is to be successful in work and contribute to the prosperity of society.
3. **Kama** means enjoying the pleasures of life in order to be happy and fulfilled. This includes enjoyment of the senses and sexual pleasure. However, restraint is needed since pleasure activities cannot bring lasting happiness or peace.
4. **Moksha** is a Hindu's ultimate aim – to be free from the cycle of **samsara** and be reunited with Brahman.

Four varnas

Hindus believe that all people are equal in the spiritual realm, but in society there are material differences that help it to work. One creation story describes how Brahma created humanity in four groups, each from a part of his body. The groups are called the **four varnas**:

1. Brahmins (priests and teachers)
2. Kshatriyas (soldiers and rulers)
3. Vaishyas (merchants and farmers)
4. Shudras (labourers and craftsmen)

This system showed that each person in society is dependent on others. The original varnas did not prevent people from doing different jobs or marrying people in a different varna.

> **Objectives**
> Understand key Hindu beliefs.

> **Key terms**
> **Dharma:** religion; the right conduct and laws that uphold order and harmony in society.
> **Artha:** economic development – the second aim of life.
> **Kama:** having a regulated sense of enjoyment and pleasure, including erotic love, in order to be healthy and fulfilled – the third aim of life.
> **Moksha (moksa):** liberation from samsara, i.e. the atman will not be reincarnated any more (Hinduism, Sikhism).
> **Samsara:** the world where the cycle of birth, death and rebirth takes place.
> **Four varnas:** the four main divisions of Hindu society: Brahmins (priests), Kshatriyas (rulers and warriors), Vaishyas (merchants and farmers) and Shudras (labourers).

A A member of the Shudra varna

B A member of the Vaishya varna

Later, the varnas were divided into a number of sub-classes or castes. A person's caste depended on birth into a particular family. Each caste had its own laws of purity, eating, marriage and social mixing. This system became open to abuse because it did not allow people equal opportunities. Aspects of the caste system were banned by the Indian government, but it is still influential in rural places.

Nowadays, the Brahmins might be considered the scholarly community, including lawyers, ministers and diplomats. The Kshatriyas include administrators, the Vaishyas include shopkeepers and businessmen, and the Shudras are the service-providing community including manual and farm labourers.

C *Should people marry someone from the same varna?*

Case study

Four stages of life

A Hindu's dharma is different depending on which stage of their life they have reached. There are four stages that apply to members of the three higher varnas. Each stage has a particular duty.

The **student** stage is after childhood when a young person must take their education seriously and study sacred texts to gain knowledge of God. When Hindus reach the **householder** stage, their dharma is to marry, raise a family and serve the community. When people retire and their family is grown up, they reach the **forest** stage. Middle-aged people have more time to reflect and meditate. In the past, some became a forest dweller (hermit) to do this. The **ascetic** stage involves leaving the family and adopting the life of a wandering holy man. The last two stages are not often practised nowadays, although older people might well meditate more and prepare for their deaths.

Activity

1. Read the case study. Explain how dharma varies depending on someone's stage of life.

Activities

2. Explain the four aims of life according to Hindus.
3. How might the goal of kama affect married couples' relationships?
4. Explain the Hindu varnas.
5. Explain how the varna system became unfair.

Beliefs and teachings

I am a bard (poet), my father is a physician, my mother's job is to grind the corn.

Rig Veda 9.112.3

Discussion activity

With a partner, in a small group or as a whole class, discuss the following statement: 'People should marry someone from the same varna in order to be happy.' Do you agree? Give reasons for your answer, showing that you have thought about more than one point of view.

AQA Examiner's tip

You need to consider how these beliefs affect the way Hindus live their lives.

Summary

You should now be able to explain key Hindu beliefs.

4.7 Muslim beliefs

The Five Pillars

The **Five Pillars** are the five essential duties every believer must fulfil.

1 Shahadah – the declaration of faith

The Shahadah sums up Muslims' belief:

> *I witness that there is no other God but Allah, and Muhammad is the Prophet of Allah.*

This declaration of faith contains the two basic concepts of tawhid (Allah's oneness) and **risalah** (belief in Allah's messengers – prophets, angels and holy books). Belief in Muhammad as the Prophet of God is known as 'rusulullah'.

2 Salah – prayer five times a day

When the muezzin calls Muslims to prayer from the minaret, he recites the Shahadah and adds, 'Come to prayer, come to security.' In the morning he says, 'Prayer is better than sleep.'

Muslims can pray in any clean place, but whenever possible they pray in mosques, particularly on Friday, the Muslim holy day. Prayers, whether performed at home or in the mosque, follow a set pattern (see pages 18 and 45).

Muslims may also use a string of prayer beads in personal (du'a) prayers when reciting the names of Allah.

3 Zakah – almsgiving

Muslims have a duty to give money to charity. Zakah means 'purity'. Giving to those in need helps to purify the heart from greed and selfishness. Once money has been deducted for essentials such as food, clothing and housing, Muslims are expected to give 2.5 per cent of the money they have left as zakah. The money goes towards helping the poor, the disabled, building hospitals or is used for religious purposes. Muslims may give other money to charity (called sadaqah), but zakah is looked upon as compulsory since all wealth and property belong to Allah, so not to give would be cheating Allah.

4 Sawm – fasting during Ramadan

Ramadan is the ninth month of the Muslim calendar, when Muhammad received the revelations in the Qur'an. During this month, Muslims over the age of 12 are expected to fast unless they are old, sick, travellers, pregnant or mothers who are breastfeeding. Younger children may take part in a partial fast. Muslims who are fasting have a meal before sunrise and then go without food and drink until sunset. During Ramadan, Muslims especially try to remember the poor and reflect on the teachings of the Qur'an. When the new moon can be seen, Muslims celebrate the end of the fast with the festival of Eid ul Fitr.

Objectives

Understand key Muslim beliefs.

Key terms

Five Pillars: the five most important duties: to pray, to give to charity, to fast and to go on pilgrimage.

Risalah: in Islam, the belief that Allah chose messengers (prophets) to speak his message, especially Muhammad.

Links

There are three main beliefs in Islam: tawhid, risalah and akhirah. See pages 79 and 93 to find out more about tawhid and akhirah respectively.

A *A Muslim man holding prayer beads*

Chapter 4 Origins and beliefs 87

B *Muslims celebrating Eid ul Fitr*

5 Hajj – pilgrimage to Makkah

During the Muslim twelfth month (Dhul Hijjah), over 2 million people make the annual pilgrimage to Makkah.

■ Ummah

The **ummah** is the worldwide community of Muslims. Muhammad established the ummah when he went to Madinah (the Hijrah) and built a mosque there. He worked for the next 10 years to unite the tribes into one community under the rule of Allah with equality for all. Practising the Five Pillars unites Muslims and confirms the Islamic vision of a single community in which everyone comes from Allah and returns to him.

Activities

1. Explain the meaning of 'risalah'.
2. How does prayer in the mosque strengthen the ummah?
3. Explain the Muslim attitude towards money. How does it differ, if at all, from your own attitude?
4. In your opinion, why do Muslims fast?

Summary

You should now be able to explain key Muslim beliefs.

∞ links

Look back to page 62 to see a detailed account of Hajj.

Discussion activity

1. With a partner or in a small group:
   a. Decide which of the Five Pillars is the most important for Muslims.
   b. Discuss the following statement: 'Praying five times a day is too difficult.'

   Give reasons for your answers.

Key terms

Ummah: all Muslims are regarded as part of a brotherhood; the nation of Islam.

AQA Examiner's tip

You need to consider how these beliefs affect the way Muslims live their lives.

4.8 Jewish beliefs

■ Shema

The **Shema** is the most important Jewish prayer. It begins:

> *Hear, O Israel: the Lord our God, the Lord is One. Love the Lord your God with all your heart and with all your soul and with all your strength.*
>
> Deuteronomy 6:4–5

These words are part of the morning and evening services and the final prayer at night. The Shema is written on a tiny scroll kept in the mezuzah, a small box fixed to a doorpost which is touched when a person enters the house or room. The belief in one God (monotheism) was what distinguished the Jews from their neighbours at the time of Abraham and Moses.

■ Principles of the faith

There is no set list of beliefs that all Jews must accept. The emphasis is more on practising the faith handed down through generations. However, Maimonides (12th century CE) summarised what came to be known as the Thirteen Principles of the Faith, which can be found in the Siddur (Jewish prayer book).

The first five principles are that:

- God is the creator of all
- God is one
- God has no body or material form
- God is eternal
- God alone is to be worshipped.

The Jewish Bible (Tenakh) opens with an account of God creating the world. Jews believe that God continues to sustain the world and act in history to influence events. He showed his saving power when he brought the Hebrew slaves out of Egypt. Because God is eternal and has no body or material form, he alone must be worshipped, no other. Jews do not make images or pictures of God, even in symbolic form.

The next four principles are that:

- God spoke through the prophets of the Tenakh
- Moses was the greatest of all prophets
- God gave Moses the Law
- The Law is complete and final.

The last four principles are that:

- God knows everything, even before it happens
- God will reward the righteous and punish sinners both in this world and the next

Objectives

Understand key Jewish beliefs.

Key terms

Shema: Jewish prayer affirming belief in one God, found in the Torah.

⚭ links

See page 93 for information about Jewish beliefs about God and the afterlife.

Look back to page 76 to remind yourself about the origins of Judaism and Abraham and Moses.

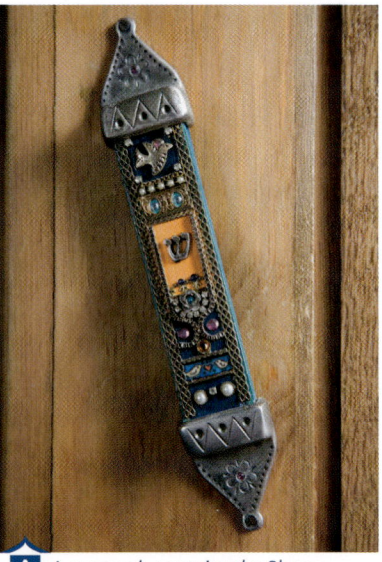

A A mezuzah contains the Shema

Activities

1. Explain how Jews keep the Shema in mind.

2. Why do Jews make no pictures or images of God?

3. What role do the prophets play in Judaism?

- God will send a **Maschiach (Messiah)** (an 'anointed' leader who will be their saviour)
- God will restore the dead to life.

The Holocaust

The Jewish belief that God acts in history and shows his saving power was severely tested during the Holocaust when 6 million Jews were killed in concentration camps by the Nazis.

Some Jews asked, 'What happened to the covenant? We obey God's laws and in return God is supposed to protect and deliver us. Where is God in Auschwitz?'

The faith of other Jews was not destroyed by the Holocaust. They believe that human freedom means that people can do truly terrible things to each other. God cannot stop them without taking away their free will. They feel that if they had stopped practising their faith, Hitler would have won. God's chosen people must survive and show the world that life can triumph over death.

B Auschwitz concentration camp

Activities

4. Read the case study. How did the Holocaust challenge Jewish people's faith in God?

5. With a partner or in a small group, discuss the two contrasting responses to the Holocaust. Which opinion do you agree with? Explain your reasons.

Discussion activity

With a partner, in a small group or as a whole class, discuss the following statement: 'If someone followed the Shema, they would not need to follow any other rules in Judaism.' Do you agree? Give reasons for your answer, showing that you have thought about more than one point of view.

Summary

You should now be able to explain key Jewish beliefs.

Key terms

Maschiach (Messiah): in Judaism, God's chosen king (anointed one) who will bring about a new age of peace in the world.

Extension activity

Write a paragraph about how a Jew could apply the Shema to daily living.

AQA Examiner's tip

You need to consider how these beliefs affect the way Jews live their lives.

4.9 Sikh beliefs

The Khalsa (community of the pure)

In 1699 CE, at the spring festival of Baisakhi (Vaisakhi), Guru Gobind Singh appeared from a tent carrying a sharp sword. He demanded a volunteer to offer his head for sacrifice. A silent fear gripped the crowd, but one man stepped forward. The Guru took him into the tent, a sickening thud was heard, and the Guru reappeared, his sword dripping with blood.

He repeated his call four more times with the same effect. The crowd thought the volunteers were dead, but the Guru returned with all five men unharmed. He gave amrit (sugar and water) to them to drink, and sprinkled it over them. They became the first members of the **Khalsa**. Sikhs still use amrit in the ceremony for those wishing to join the Khalsa.

> **Objectives**
> Understand key Sikh beliefs.

> **Key terms**
> **Khalsa:** the Sikh community, founded by Guru Gobind Singh in 1699 CE. Literally 'the community of the pure'.
> **Five Ks:** five symbols worn by Sikhs: uncut hair (kesh), steel bangle (kara), wooden comb (kangha), sword (kirpan) and white shorts (kachera).

> **Activities**
> 1. Why is the Khalsa important for Sikhs?
> 2. How prepared would you be to give your life for your beliefs?

A *The spring festival of Baisakhi*

The Five Ks

When the Khalsa began, Guru Gobind Singh instructed all members of the Sikh brotherhood to wear the **Five Ks** to bind the Khalsa together and to symbolise their faith.

The kachera

The kachera is a white cotton undergarment, worn by both men and women. It must not come below the knee. Its loose fit allows freedom of movement to fight, if necessary, for what is right. It reminds Sikhs to live a pure and moral life.

The kangha

The kangha is a small wooden comb that symbolises a clean body and mind, reminding Sikhs to 'untangle' themselves from impure thoughts and evil.

The kara

The kara is a steel bangle worn on the right arm or wrist. Its unbroken circle is a symbol of God's eternal nature and the unity of the Khalsa. It reminds Sikhs that their actions must be worthy of being a Sikh.

The kesh

Kesh is the Sikh's uncut hair, a symbol of holiness and strength. Sikhs promise not to cut their hair but let it grow as a symbol of their faith, commitment and obedience to God. Men wear turbans and women wear scarves to keep their hair tidy. Men must not trim their beards. Women must not cut any body hair or pluck their eyebrows.

B *Monty Panesar, the first Sikh England cricketer, wears the kesh but covers his hair with a scarf when playing cricket*

The kirpan

The kirpan is a ceremonial sword. It can be from a few centimetres to nearly a metre in length. Most Sikhs now wear a tiny one as a symbol of dignity and self-respect. It reminds Sikhs that they must fight a spiritual battle, uphold the truth and defend the weak and oppressed.

In Britain, some Sikhs choose not to wear the Five Ks. Some may shave their beards or choose to wear only the kara. However, the Five Ks remain an important symbol of their faith and unity in the Khalsa.

Kurahit (prohibitions)

Members of the Khalsa are also required to keep four prohibitions relating to their personal conduct. These are set out in the Rahit Maryada (the Sikh code of discipline) and are known as the Kurahit.

Sikhism emphasises what you should do, rather than what you should not. The Gurus taught that true religion meant acting righteously by worshipping God, earning an honest living, and sharing what you have with others.

links

See page 101 to find out more about the Kurahit.

Research activity

Using the internet or a library, find out how Sikhs join the Khalsa today.

Activities

3 Explain the religious symbolism of each of the Five Ks.

4 Why might some Sikhs in Britain not wish to wear all the Five Ks?

Extension activity

Write a paragraph about how Sikh beliefs described here affect their day-to-day lives.

Discussion activity

With a partner, in a small group or as a whole class, discuss the following statement: 'Wearing special religious clothing is not good for community cohesion.' Do you agree? Give reasons for your answer, showing that you have thought about more than one point of view.

AQA Examiner's tip

You need to consider how these beliefs affect the way Sikhs live their lives.

Summary

You should now be able to explain key Sikh beliefs.

4.10 The soul and the afterlife

What is the goal of life?

All religions look forward to a time of perfect peace and happiness that can be reached by living a good life. Most religions, except Buddhism, believe that people have a **soul** that lives on after they die.

Buddhism, Hinduism and Sikhism

For these religions, life is locked in a cycle of birth, death and rebirth (samsara). The goal of life is to gain release from samsara and reach eternal peace. Doing good deeds to gain merit determines how a person is reborn (**kamma (karma)**).

Buddhism

Buddhists believe that there is no permanent part of a person (a soul) that lives on after death. Living skilfully results in good kamma helping **rebirth**. The actual person is not reborn but their karmic energy sets another life in motion. The goal of life is to achieve nibbana ('blown out' like a candle), a state of eternal peace and happiness, beyond life's suffering and impermanence.

Hinduism

Hindus believe that Brahman is present in each person as **atman** (soul) that is eternal and pure spirit. When the body dies, the atman takes on another body and returns to another life (**reincarnation**) depending on a person's **karma**. A Hindu's goal is union with the Supreme Reality (Brahman) through moksha.

Sikhism

Sikhs believe that each person has an immortal soul, a 'divine spark' that is part of God and will be reabsorbed into God after liberation (mukti) from samsara. At death, the soul is reincarnated into another body, depending on karma. The goal of life is to be reunited with God.

Christianity, Islam and Judaism

Christianity

For Christians, the soul is spiritual and immortal. Christians believe that Jesus rose from the dead. They believe in the **resurrection of the body**, the idea that each person will, in some recognisable form, have life after death. God will decide on **Judgement Day** whether they will go to **heaven** or **hell**, depending on their faith and deeds. Roman Catholics also believe in **purgatory**. Some Christians believe that at the end of time, Jesus will return for a final judgement and the dead will rise, restored to glorified bodies.

Objectives

Explore beliefs about the soul (or no soul).

Explore beliefs about the afterlife and how this life influences it.

links

Look back to page 84 to remind yourself of what is meant by moksha.

Key terms

Soul: the spiritual part of a person that continues after death.

Kamma (karma): literally 'action'; deliberate actions that affect the believer's circumstances in this and future lives; cause and effect (Buddhism).

Rebirth: being born again.

Atman: self. Can refer to the body, mind or soul depending on context. Usually the inner, or real, self (Hinduism).

Reincarnation: being reborn again in another form.

Karma: the law of cause and effect (Hinduism). That a person reaps what they sow (Sikhism).

Resurrection of the body: the belief that God will raise everyone to life before the Judgement. Life after this will be in a perfect body that does not die.

Judgement Day: the time when God will decide whether people go to heaven or hell.

Heaven: eternal life with God.

Hell: eternal separation from God.

Purgatory: a place where souls go to be purified from their sins before they go to heaven.

A Paradise is often imagined as a beautiful garden

Islam

Muslims call life after death **akhirah**. Muslims believe that the soul is questioned by the angel of death and taken to a place of waiting (**barzakh**) until Judgement Day when all bodies will be raised to life again. Allah **sorts** the souls by making them cross the hair-narrow **Sirat Bridge** that spans the fires of hell. Good people are transported across the path quickly and are led to **Paradise**.

Judaism

Jews believe that the soul is part of a person, not something separate. Jewish ideas about an afterlife vary. The Bible speaks of **Sheol**, a place where the dead go. Jews hope for resurrection and immortality. Many believe in Judgement Day when people must account for their actions to God. Sinners will be sent to Sheol for cleansing before entering God's presence. Jews look forward to the resurrection of the dead in the Messianic Age, when the Messiah will reign.

Activities

1. How would you answer the question, 'What is the goal of life?'
2. Explain beliefs about life after death in each of the two religions you are studying.
3. For each of the two religions you are studying, explain how their beliefs about life after death might affect the way they treat other people and live their lives.

Summary

You should now be able to explain religious ideas about the existence of a soul and life after death.

AQA Examiner's tip

Make sure that you know the key terms listed here for the religions you are studying. You also need to be able to explain how these beliefs affect the way believers live their lives.

Key terms

Akhirah: everlasting life after death.

Barzakh: state of waiting for Judgement Day.

Sorting: the separation of those who are sent to Hell from those who are sent to Paradise on Judgement Day (Islam).

Sirat Bridge: the pathway to Paradise that crosses over Hell. People cross it at different speeds according to their actions in this life. Some fall from it into Hell (Islam).

Paradise: place of perfect happiness; the afterlife.

Sheol: the world of the dead (Judaism).

Discussion activity

1. With a partner, in a small group or as a whole class, discuss the following statements:

   a 'No one can see a person's soul, therefore it does not exist.'

   b 'Life after death is just wishful thinking.'

   Do you agree? Give reasons for your answers, showing that you have thought about more than one point of view.

Assessment guidance

4

Origins and beliefs – summary

With reference to at least **two** of the religions you have studied, for the examination you should now be able to:

✔ describe the origins of the faith, including the life of the founder or prophet

✔ evaluate the importance of the life of the founder or prophet to believers

✔ explain the concept of God (or no God)

✔ describe and explain the nature of the afterlife, and how this life influences it

✔ explain the concept of soul (or similar) or no soul

✔ describe and explain the basic beliefs and teachings of the religion

✔ evaluate the importance of the beliefs and teachings of the religion to believers and the impact they have on the way they live their lives.

AQA Examiner's tip Remember that you must refer to the origins and beliefs of two religions in the examination.

Sample answer

1 Write an answer to the following examination question:

'Founders and prophets lived so long ago that they are no longer relevant today.'
Do you agree? Give reasons for your answer, showing that you have thought about more than one point of view. Refer to religious arguments in your answer.

(6 marks)

2 Read the following sample answer:

> People who do not follow a religion might not see the relevance of a prophet who lived long ago because they think of them as just characters in history. Some prophets, like Moses, were supposed to do miracles, like parting the Red Sea. Many people today think that is impossible, so they begin to doubt whether accounts of their lives are true. But, for a Jew, Moses is very relevant to today because he gave the Jewish law that all Jews follow. His leadership brought them out of slavery to freedom, something which Jews today value very much. If it weren't for Moses, they would not have reached the Promised Land and become a nation.

3 With a partner, discuss the sample answer. Do you think that there are other things that the student could have included in the answer?

4 What mark would you give this answer out of 6? (Look at the mark scheme in the Introduction on page 7 (A02) before you attempt this.) What are the reasons for the mark you have given?

AQA Examination-style questions

1 Read the statement and answer the following questions.

> **66** *Religious beliefs are communicated through founders and prophets.* **99**

(a) Outline the major events in the life of the founder or prophet in **one** religion. *(6 marks)*

(b) Explain briefly **one** belief held by a religion different from the one used in part (a). *(3 marks)*

(c) 'There is no God in control of the universe.' What do you think? Explain your opinion. *(3 marks)*

(d) 'Belief in life after death gives meaning to a person's life.'
Do you agree? Give reasons for your answer, showing that you have thought about more than one point of view. Refer to religious arguments in your answer. *(6 marks)*

> **AQA Examiner's tip**
> Remember that when you are given a statement and asked 'do you agree?' you must show what you think and the reasons why other people might take a different view. If your answer is one sided, you can only achieve a maximum of 4 marks. If you make no comment about religious belief or practice, you will achieve no more than 3 marks.

5 Practices and belonging

5.1 Introduction: Buddhist and Christian behaviour codes and duties

Joining a religious group means that a person is expected to behave in a way that matches the religion's beliefs or code of conduct. Each religion has its own set of rules and regulations or principles for living. Those who belong to the faith are encouraged as a matter of duty to live in accordance with those rules and to take part in religious practices. Those who do not keep to the rules may be encouraged to repent, be warned about their behaviour or, in extreme cases, excluded from the faith; for example, Roman Catholics have excluded people from the Church (excommunication).

Buddhism

The Three Refuges and the bodhisattva vow

Buddhist meetings open with the recitation of the **Three Refuges** (the Three Jewels). These are available to help Buddhists reach nibbana. 'I go to the Buddha for my refuge. I go to the dharma [teaching] for my refuge and I go to the sangha [Buddhist community] for my refuge.' Buddhists follow the Buddha's teaching as they believe it shows the way to enlightenment, and the sangha offers the ideal conditions to help them achieve their goal. In Mahayana Buddhism, a person who has already achieved a considerable degree of enlightenment may take the **bodhisattva vows**. This means that they will promise to help others to achieve enlightenment, escape the cycle of samsara and reach nibbana. The vows include promising to help save living beings, to eliminate afflictions and delusions, to learn teachings and to follow the way of the Buddha. They are taught to show compassion and loving kindness (**metta**) towards all life.

The Buddha taught that suffering is caused by desire and craving. His teachings encourage his followers to end this desire and to avoid wanting to live a life of luxury and self-indulgence, or a life of self-denial by following the Middle Way and the Noble Eightfold Path.

> **Beliefs and teachings**
>
> A man who gives way to pleasure will be swept away by craving and his thoughts will make him suffer, like waves.
>
> *Dhammapada* 339

Objectives

Introduce religious behaviour codes and duties.

Understand Buddhist and Christian codes of behaviour.

A *Religions have laws that forbid certain actions*

Key terms

Three Refuges: Buddhist bhikkhus and bhikkhunis 'take refuge' in three things: the Buddha, the Dhamma and the Sangha (the Three Jewels).

Bodhisattva vows: the bodhisattva vows to lead all beings into nibbana and to enter nibbana only after all beings have been liberated.

Metta: loving kindness. A pure love, which is not possessive and which does not seek to gain (Buddhism).

Tithing: giving a tenth of one's income to charity or to support the religion.

The Five Moral Precepts

The Buddha gave Five Moral Precepts for lay (ordinary) people to live by in order to obtain good kamma (karma):

1. Not to cause harm by physical actions.
2. Not to cause harm by actions of speech (lying, harsh words, etc.).
3. Not to cause harm through sexual activity.
4. Not to steal or take what is not given.
5. Not to take intoxicants (e.g. alcohol and drugs).

The monastic code

Buddhist monks (bhikkhus) and nuns (bhikkhunis) also have a monastic code to follow, consisting of a large number of additional rules. These include rules relating to meal times and forbidding entertainments, luxuries and the acceptance of money.

Christianity

The Ten Commandments form the basis for the behaviour codes and duties of both Christians and Jews. The account in Exodus implies that they are so important because the author is God. He gave the laws to Moses on Mount Sinai. The commandments are repeated twice in the Old Testament – Exodus 20:2–17 and Deuteronomy 5:6–21. Anything repeated twice is regarded as exceptionally important in Jewish culture. Jesus was a Jew, and Christians follow these laws and their code of behaviour is based on them and on Jesus' teachings.

The first four commandments refer to a person's duty to God and the others to other people. Jesus summed up these commandments in two parts. First, love God (the most important commandment) and, secondly, love your neighbour as yourself (Mark 12:29–31). 'Loving your neighbour' is known as the Golden Rule and is the basis for the Christian way of life and Christian compassion. This is often shown through tithing.

Activities

1. What are the Three Refuges and the bodhisattva vows?
2. Explain why the Ten Commandments are important to both Christians and Jews.
3. '"Do not harm anything" should be the most important commandment.' What do you think? Explain your opinion.

Summary

You should now be able to explain and evaluate Buddhist behaviour codes and duties, and the importance of the Ten Commandments for Christians and Jews.

links

Look back to page 80 for an explanation of the Middle Way and the Noble Eightfold Path.

Extension activity

Using the internet, find out more about the Buddhist monastic code. Record your findings.

B *The Ten Commandments*

C *The Ten Commandments in abbreviated form*

1. Worship no other gods.
2. Make no idols.
3. Do not misuse God's name.
4. Keep the Sabbath Day holy.
5. Honour your parents.
6. Do not kill.
7. Do not commit adultery.
8. Do not steal.
9. Do not lie.
10. Do not covet.

AQA Examiner's tip

Make sure that you can quote some examples of the rules, duties and/or codes from the religions you are studying.

Discussion activity

With a partner, in a small group or as a class, discuss the Ten Commandments or the Five Moral Precepts. Put them in order of importance for you. Give reasons for your selection.

5.2 Hindu and Muslim behaviour codes and duties

Hinduism

Hindu scriptures contain many virtues, which believers are encouraged to develop in their lives as they are believed to produce good karma. These include **ahimsa**, **cleanliness**, **compassion**, **honesty**, **respect**, **tolerance** and **wisdom**. Hindus are encouraged to try to avoid receiving negative karma, as it will have consequences in this life and/or the next.

- **Ahimsa:** Hindus are forbidden to use violence that might harm living creatures. To do so brings negative karmic consequences, whereas to avoid violence brings positive karma. The concept of ahimsa was very much in Gandhi's mind when he used peaceful non-cooperation in his quest for freedom for the people of India. He did not use violent methods.
- **Cleanliness** is important for good health, but it is also a virtue to have inner cleanliness. This is obtained through devotions and worship of God, being selfless, non-violent and cultivating all the other virtues.
- **Compassion** may be shown through giving help and selfless service to others, including donating to charity.
- Hindus are expected to be **honest** with their family, friends and everyone with whom they have dealings, and themselves.
- **Respect** and reverence for their elders and teachers and respect for the earth and the environment are encouraged.
- Showing **tolerance** towards others and everything is regarded as the right action, as is showing respect towards those who have **wisdom** and who teach in love.

Islam

Muslims are taught to obey Allah and to remember his will in all they do.

Muslim morality is based on the Qur'an and the **Hadith**, and the virtues of courage, fairness, generosity, kindness, mercy, purity, sympathy and truthfulness are regarded as noble qualities. Such teachings as the Hadith, 'He who eats and drinks while his brother goes hungry, is not one of us' help to shape the way a Muslim behaves. Muslims have a legal framework known as Shari'ah, which is based on the Qur'an, the Hadith and precedent (past judgements). It deals with commerce, family, hygiene, politics, sexuality and social issues. Punishments are given for breaking rules such as drinking alcohol, unlawful sexual intercourse and theft.

Objectives

Understand Hindu and Muslim behaviour codes and duties and their importance for believers.

Key terms

Ahimsa: not killing. Respect for life, not being violent (Hinduism).

Cleanliness: keeping free from impurities and anything that is dishonourable.

Compassion: loving kindness. A feeling of sympathy that makes one want to help.

Honesty: being truthful and just, not cheating or stealing.

Respect: showing consideration for others' feelings, views or beliefs.

Tolerance: willingness to permit other views, beliefs and opinions.

Wisdom: showing soundness of judgement.

Hadith: sayings of the Prophet Muhammad. A major source of Islamic Law.

Beliefs and teachings

The most honourable among you in the sight of God is the one who is most God-conscious.

Qur'an 49:13

links

See page 131 to find out more about Shari'ah.

Look back to pages 86–87 for further information on the Five Pillars of Islam.

The Five Pillars of Islam

The main duties of a Muslim are summed up in the Five Pillars of Islam.

1. **Shahadah:** The first duty is to declare and publicly confess belief that there is no God but Allah and that Muhammad is his prophet.
2. **Salah:** Muslims take part in ritual prayer five times a day.
3. **Zakat:** Muslims are taught that all wealth belongs to God and at least 2.5 per cent of a person's net income must be paid to the mosque each year. Wealth is purified by the tax, which helps the needy and the upkeep of the mosque.
4. **Sawm:** Adult Muslims (unless exempt, for example through pregnancy, illness or old age) are required to fast from dawn to sunset each day during the month of Ramadan. This is a physical and spiritual discipline that exercises self-control and involves studying the Qur'an with the aim of getting closer to Allah.
5. **Hajj:** Every Muslim should try to go on pilgrimage at least once in a lifetime.

A *Hajj is a once-in-a-lifetime experience*

AQA Examiner's tip

Make sure that you are able to discuss why religious believers are concerned about good behaviour, and what this means in the religions you have chosen.

Discussion activity

With a partner, in a small group or as a class, discuss which you regard as the most important Muslim practice. Give reasons for your opinion.

Activities

1. Choose **five** of the virtues in Hinduism and explain what they are and their importance.
2. Explain the sources used by Muslims to help guide them in their behaviour and actions.
3. 'Ahimsa is the most important Hindu virtue.' What do you think? Explain your opinion.

Summary

You should now be able to explain the religious virtues for Hindus, and the role of the Hadith, Shari'ah and the Five Pillars in setting out the behaviour rules and duties for Muslims.

5.3 Jewish and Sikh behaviour codes and duties

Judaism

Being a devout Jew is a complete way of life as all actions from getting dressed in the morning to going to bed at night are part of worship. In addition to the Ten Commandments, Jews have many laws, including what they should wear. For example:

> *You shall make tassels on the corners of your garments, with a blue cord on each tassel. You will have these tassels to look at and so you will remember all the commands of the Lord.*
>
> Numbers 15:38–9

In the Torah, there are 613 **mitzvot** consisting of '365 negative commandments like the number of days in the solar year, and 248 positive commandments' (*Talmud*). Topics that the mitzvot cover include God, the Torah, signs and symbols, prayers and blessings, love and brotherhood, the poor and unfortunate, the treatment of gentiles (non-Jews), marriage, divorce and the family, forbidden sexual practices, times and seasons, dietary laws, business practices, employees, servants and slaves, vows, oaths and swearing, Sabbath and Jubilee laws, courts and criminal law, agriculture and animal husbandry, idolatry, clothing, the Temple and war. Not all the mitzvot are appropriate for today, as some refer to the sacrifices and services in the Temple (it was destroyed by the Romans) and others concerning criminal law would only be possible in a Jewish religious state. Some groups of Jews take the keeping of the mitzvot more seriously than others, but the following six are regarded as very important:

1. To believe in God, the creator of all things.
2. Not to believe in anything else other than God.
3. To believe in God's Oneness.
4. To fear God.
5. To love God.
6. Not to pursue the passions of your heart.

Every week, Jews celebrate Shabbat (Sabbath). It is an extremely important celebration for Jews as it observes the fourth commandment (Exodus 20:8–11), which is to keep the Sabbath Day holy.

It is also a duty for Jews to treat people fairly and with justice. This is known as **tzedek**:

> *Follow justice and justice alone.*
>
> Deuteronomy 16:20

Objectives

Understand Jewish and Sikh behaviour codes and duties and their importance for believers.

A Torah scroll

Key terms

Mitzvot: in Judaism, the commandments that are in God's Law (the Torah). There are 613 in total.

Tzedek: an act of charity that combines fairness and compassion (Judaism).

Kurahit: things which are not allowed – prohibitions (Sikhism).

Sewa (seva): acts of service and charity to members of the Sangat or others (Sikhism).

Research activity

Using the internet or a library, find out about Jewish practices on Shabbat. Record your findings.

links

Look back to pages 46–47 for information about Jewish worship on Shabbat.

Extension activity

Using the internet, find out more examples of the 613 mitzvot.

Chapter 5 Practices and belonging

■ Sikhism

Khalsa (baptised) Sikhs are taught in the Rahit Maryada (code of conduct) to wear the Five Ks and recite prayers five times each day. They are also given four 'do nots', which are known as the **Kurahit** prohibitions:

1. Do not cut the hair (includes shaving).
2. Do not use tobacco or any other intoxicants like alcohol and non-medical drugs.
3. Do not commit adultery.
4. Do not eat meat that has been ritually slaughtered.

B *Khalsa Sikhs are easily recognisable because they wear turbans*

They also have five virtues, which are important qualities that Sikhs are encouraged to develop so that they can break free from the cycle of birth, life, death and rebirth. These positive qualities are truth (Sat), compassion (Daya), contentment (Santokh), humility (Nimrata) and love (Pyare).

Sikhs also believe in equality and behaving honourably towards others.

All Sikhs are expected to perform **sewa** (selfless service) to help the community. Much is done in the gurdwara by helping in the langar (kitchen), cleaning the floors, etc., but the wider community benefits as well. Sikhs may do voluntary work in hospitals, care homes, community centres and other such places. The Guru Granth Sahib encourages such actions:

> 66 *One who performs selfless service, without thought of reward, shall attain his Lord and Master.* 99
>
> Guru Granth Sahib 286

Guru Ram Das developed the Sikh system of tithing. Traditionally, it is to give one-tenth of one's income to support Sikhism and good works, but many people give what they can afford. Sikhs believe that spiritually it brings benefit in relation to karma, as tithing is a positive thing to do.

Beliefs and teachings

Practise truth, contentment and kindness; this is the most excellent way of life. One who is so blessed by the Formless Lord God renounces selfishness, and becomes the dust of all.

Guru Granth Sahib 51

∞ links

Look back to page **96** to remind yourself of what is meant by tithing.

AQA Examiner's tip

Make sure that you are able to explain how following these codes helps a person feel that they belong to, and are part of, the religion.

Activities

1. Give **five** examples of the topics included in the 613 mitzvot.
2. Why do you think the four Kurahit are important for Sikhs?
3. 'If people cannot afford to tithe, they should provide sewa (unpaid service) instead.' What do you think? Explain your opinion.

Discussion activity

With a partner, in a small group or as a class, discuss whether you think rules made thousands of years ago can be appropriate for today. Give specific examples to support the reasons for your answer.

Summary

You should now be able to explain what is meant by the mitzvot in Judaism, and the Kurahit, virtues, sewa and tithing in Sikhism, and evaluate their importance as part of a code of behaviour.

5.4 Dietary laws

Members of minority religions sometimes have difficulty in keeping dietary laws in Britain because the required foods may not be readily available locally.

Buddhism

Many Buddhists are vegetarians because of the principle of not harming living creatures (First Precept). Animals are part of the samsara cycle so, although meat eating is allowed, vegetarianism is encouraged. The Buddha advised monks to avoid eating boars, dogs, elephants, horses, humans, hyenas, lions, snakes and tigers. However, monks and nuns eat meat if it is offered, but they must not kill it themselves. They rely on alms (charitable donations) and it would be disrespectful to reject what they are given.

Christianity

Most Christians eat meat, although some choose to be vegetarians because they do not wish animals to be killed. The book of Genesis suggests that humans were originally vegetarians, but after the great flood God said to Noah:

> " Everything that lives and moves will be food for you.
> Just as I gave you the green plants, I now give you everything. "
>
> *Genesis 9:3*

Acts 10:9–15 records how God gave Peter permission in a vision to eat creatures that he thought were unclean. Paul also said, 'Do not let anyone judge you by what you eat' (Colossians 2:16). Many Christians campaign for the humane treatment of animals. Some see organic and free-range methods of farming as being good stewardship.

Hinduism

Hindus believe in the sacredness of all life, reincarnation and the principle of ahimsa (non-violence), so most are vegetarians. Inflicting pain and suffering on animals is believed to have negative karmic consequences. Eating meat is not prohibited, but camels, crabs, ducks, pork and snails are usually avoided. The cow is sacred to Hindus, so beef is not allowed. However, products such as milk, yoghurt and butter are thought to promote purity of body, mind and spirit, so are eaten.

Islam

Most Muslims eat meat, but animals have to be killed in the name of Allah so the meat is **halal** (lawful or permitted). Animals or poultry are slaughtered in a ritual way known as Zibah. This involves severing the jugular vein, carotid artery and windpipe by a single cut with a sharp knife and draining all the blood.

Objectives
Know and understand the food laws of the different faiths.

Key terms
Halal: meat that is prepared in the correct way for Muslims to eat.
Haram: something that is forbidden to a Muslim, e.g. pork.
Kashrut: laws relating to having a kosher lifestyle.
Kosher: food that conforms to Jewish dietary laws.

Activities
1 Explain the food laws for the religion(s) you are studying.

2 'All foods that are good for your health should be allowed.' What do you think? Explain your opinion.

Beliefs and teachings
He hath forbidden you only carrion, and blood, and swineflesh, and that which hath been immolated [offered as a sacrifice] to (the name of) any other than Allah.

Qur'an 2:173

Research activity
Using the internet or a library, find out more about halal meat and/or kosher food.

Prohibited meat is called **haram** and includes pig meat and any animal that was dead.

Judaism

The **Kashrut** dietary laws involve not eating non-kosher food, but many Reform Jews regard the laws as being outdated as most were instigated for hygiene reasons. Orthodox Jews regard them as God-given to test their obedience and to mark out the Jewish people as different from other nations (Leviticus 20:26). An animal that is **kosher** 'has a split hoof completely divided and chews the cud' (Leviticus 11:3). So beef, deer, goats, lamb and sheep may be eaten but not camel, pigs and rabbits. Animals must be ritually slaughtered (Deuteronomy 12:21) and the blood drained. Poultry may be eaten, but not birds of prey which are trayf (forbidden). Seafood with fins and scales are kosher but not insects. A Jewish kitchen has two sinks, sets of cutlery, etc., because meat and dairy products may not be mixed or eaten at the same meal:

> *Do not cook a young goat in its mother's milk.*
> Exodus 23:19

Sikhism

Although many Sikhs are vegetarians, they may eat meat because:

> *All food is pure, for God has provided it for our sustenance.*
> Guru Granth Sahib 472

The Kurahit forbids them to eat ritually killed meat, such as halal and kosher meat. Some Sikhs do not eat beef or pork because of the social environment in which they have been brought up. The food in the langar is vegetarian, so no one is upset by what is served.

A *Preparing food in the Golden Temple, Amritsar*

Discussion activity

With a partner, in a small group or as a class, discuss the challenges dietary laws may present in a multicultural society. Make notes on the key points to use as examples in the examination.

AQA Examiner's tip

In most religions there is a diversity in the practice of believers. Include examples when answering questions.

Summary

You should now be able to explain the dietary laws for the religions you are studying.

5.5 Prayer and meditation

Prayer and meditation are important practices in each of the major world religions.

Buddhism

Buddhists believe that the value of prayer is that it helps the mind find its own natural strength and wisdom. Unlike the other major religions, Buddhists are not praying to a god, but prayer helps them make decisions and deal with problems. Buddhists meditate because it is an important part of their path towards obtaining enlightenment and reaching nibbana. Various techniques are used to develop concentration, insight, mindfulness and tranquillity. Samatha meditation is used in order to gain a feeling of calm where the mind is focused on one object or thing. Vipassana meditation is used to show the true nature of things, such as problems that may result from craving and ignorance.

Christianity

Prayer is seen as vital in the Christian life, and many use the words of the Lord's Prayer that Jesus taught his disciples as part of their prayer time: 'Our Father, who art in heaven…' (see Luke 11:2–4). Christians also meditate upon words from the Bible as part of their devotions, as they regard it as God's Word. Christian mystics believe that, through seeking God, it is possible to have direct experience of God. Christian mysticism is about the union of God with human beings through the Holy Spirit living within a person. Paul wrote:

> *I have been crucified with Christ and I no longer live, but Christ lives in me.*
>
> Galatians 12:20

Paul even talks about experiencing heaven.

The goal of the Christian mystic is to become like Jesus Christ, closely united with God.

Hinduism

Yoga meditation, including **karma yoga**, **jnana**, **astanga** and **bhakti yoga**, is important in a Hindu's quest to reach moksha (release).

- **Karma yoga** involves working or performing service without seeking to be rewarded. Most yoga ashrams (places of religious retreat) have times for karma yoga when those staying at the ashram are able to do unpaid jobs.
- **Jnana yoga** involves following the path of seeking to develop intellect and spiritual knowledge and wisdom.
- **Astanga yoga** is energetic and incorporates traditional yoga positions, which are designed to stretch, strengthen and detoxify

Objectives

Investigate prayer and meditation practices for the religions studied.

Key terms

Prayer: words of praise, thanks or sorrow etc. offered to God or to the gods.

Meditation: a special form of concentration or prayer which uses very few or no words.

Mysticism: using prayer and meditation to achieve such a close relationship with God that the person is not aware of him/herself any more.

Karma yoga: the path of selfless service (Hinduism).

Jnana: the path of yoga based on knowledge and insight.

Astanga: yoga that develops breath awareness.

Bhakti yoga: love, devotion; one of the most common forms of yoga.

Beliefs and teachings

I know that this man – whether in the body or apart from the body I do not know, but God knows – was caught up to paradise. He heard inexpressible things, things that man is not permitted to tell.

2 Corinthians 12:3–4

links

Look back to Chapter 2 for details about forms and types of prayer and meditation for each religion.

the body. It includes techniques to calm the mind and is used particularly by those who work on their mental, physical and emotional wellbeing while getting a good workout.
- **Bhakti yoga** is the yoga of devotion, worship and focused love. The focus may be on a deity or a personal Guru.

Islam

Private prayer or **du'a** is important in Islam as it is regarded as one of the greatest acts of worship:

> *There is nothing more noble in the sight of God than du'a.*
> Hadith

It means to 'call out' to Allah, which is one of the commands given to Muslims in the Qur'an:

> *And your Lord says: 'Call on Me; I will answer your (Prayer)!'*
> Qur'an 40:60

A Yoga

Key terms

Du'a: personal prayer (Islam).
Nit nem: daily specified prayers (Sikhism).

Judaism

Most Jews pray three times a day and may use a siddur (prayer book). Private prayer is seen as important, and before meals a blessing is said over what they eat and drink. For example, before drinking wine a Jew would say (in Hebrew), 'Blessed are You – the Lord our God, King of the universe, who creates the fruit of the vine.'

Sikhism

Nit nem are daily prayers that begin with Japji Sahib and are written in a Gutka (prayer book). 'Nit' means daily and 'nem' means rule so 'nit nem' means 'daily practice'. It is a duty as it is part of the Rahit Maryada (Sikh code of conduct) and it consists of recitations from scripture and meditating on God's name. It is performed early each morning and after sunset each evening.

AQA Examiner's tip

Make sure that you learn the meaning of the technical terms regarding prayer and meditation for the religions you are studying.

Activities

1. Summarise the information given in this chapter for the religions you are studying.
2. 'Prayer is the most important religious practice.' What do you think? Explain your opinion.

Discussion activity

With a partner, in a small group or as a class, compare and contrast prayer and meditation in each religion. List the similarities and differences.

Summary

You should now be able to explain the prayer and meditation practices for the religions you are studying.

5.6 Rites of passage: birth and initiation ceremonies

Each religion has its own **rites of passage**.

Buddhism

At the birth of a child, Buddhists generally follow local customs. Parents may name their child in the local temple while a monk sprinkles it with water and blesses it. A candle is lit and the wax drips into a bowl of water. This symbolises the union of elements and the harmony that the child will aim for in life.

In Theravada Buddhism, some boys become a novice monk for a short time.

Christianity

At an infant **baptism** or **christening** the priest pours water on the baby's head and says, 'I baptise you in the name of the Father, and of the Son and of the Holy Spirit.' It symbolises new life, cleansing from sin and admission to the Church, and godparents make promises on behalf of the child. Some have a dedication service instead of infant baptism, as they believe that children should make the choice for themselves. Believers can be baptised as adults. Believers' baptism includes full immersion in a pool, symbolising cleansing from sin and being born again in Christ.

Confirmation or membership ceremonies confirm the promises made during infant baptism. A bishop usually takes the service and the individual believes that they receive the gift of the Holy Spirit through the laying on of hands. Roman Catholics anoint each person with oil.

> **Objectives**
> Investigate birth and initiation ceremonies.

> **Key terms**
> **Rites of passage:** ceremonies associated with the major moments in life such as birth, marriage and death.
> **Initiation:** being entered formally into a religion.

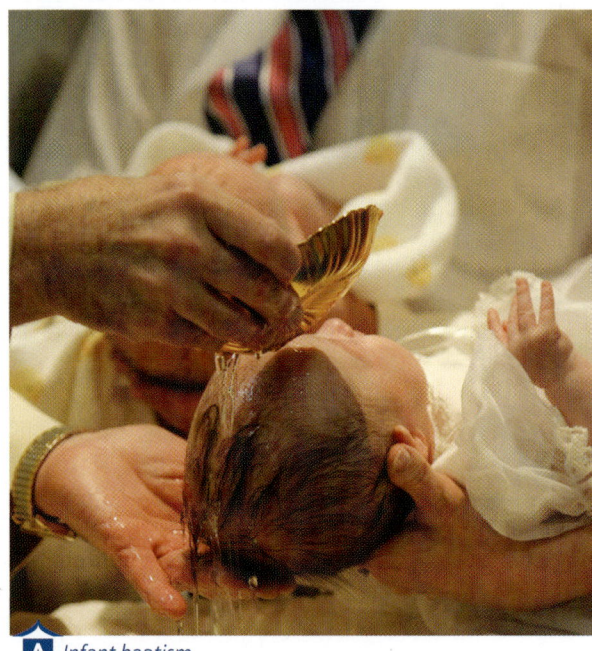

A Infant baptism

B A pool for believers' baptism

Hinduism

Some Hindus purify the baby by washing, and 10–12 days after birth a priest says prayers and announces the baby's name. For boys, the **Upanayana** initiation ceremony is performed when they reach puberty. The head is shaved and the boy receives the sacred thread, which crosses the left shoulder and goes under the right arm.

Some Hindus follow the four **ashrams**. The first ashram (stage) in a person's life involves the **brahmachari** (student) living with a spiritual teacher. They learn spiritual values and virtues and live a simple life, free from seeking pleasure, and they serve their spiritual teacher, for example by collecting alms for them.

Islam

The father whispers the Adhan (Muslim call to prayer) in the ear of the newborn baby. Then something sweet like sugar or a date is put on the baby's tongue. After seven days, the **Aqiqah** (birth) ceremony takes place. This involves shaving the baby's head, naming the child and donating to the poor. For boys, khitan (circumcision) may take place any time after eight days. At the age of four years, four months and four days, the **Bismillah** initiation ceremony occurs. This marks the start of the child's religious education.

Judaism

A Jewish boy has the **Brit Milah** (circumcision ceremony) when eight days old. This recalls the covenant that God made with Abraham. A special circumciser (mohel) carries out the operation and blesses the child. The child is named and some wine placed on his lips and a celebration follows. Now the baby is seen as religiously pure and a part of God's chosen people – the Jews. Girls aged 12 have the **Bat Mitzvah** initiation ceremony and become a 'daughter of the commandment'. Boys have their **Bar Mitzvah** aged 13 and become a 'son of the commandment', taking on the responsibilities associated with being a Jew.

Sikhism

Children are named after opening the Guru Granth Sahib. The first letter on the page becomes the first letter of the child's name. Amrit (water and sugar) is placed on the baby's lips and prayers are said to commit the child to God's grace and welcome it into the Sikh community. Everyone shares karah parshad (food) at the end of the ceremony. In later life, Sikhs may become members of the Khalsa by going through an initiation ceremony.

Summary
You should now be able to explain what happens at the birth and initiation ceremonies for the religions you are studying, and their importance.

Research activity
Using the internet or a library, find out more about the birth and initiation ceremonies for the religions you are studying.

AQA Examiner's tip
It would be useful to be able to compare and contrast the ceremonies for the religions you are studying.

Discussion activity
With a partner, in a small group or as a class, discuss the purpose and value of the birth and initiation ceremonies for the religions you are studying. Make notes on the opinions given, and the reasons for them.

Activities
1. Explain what happens at the birth and initiation ceremonies for the religions you are studying, and their importance.
2. 'Initiation ceremonies are the best way to show that a person belongs to a religion.' What do you think? Explain your opinion.

5.7 Rites of passage: marriages and funerals

■ Buddhism

In Theravada marriages, a cotton thread may be tied around the Buddha-rupa (statue) and everyone present. Monks read scriptures and bless the couple. The cotton is cut and tied around the bride and groom's wrist. In Thailand, the marriage ceremony takes place in the home, where candles are lit and incense burnt. Guests receive a flower as they sign a book of good wishes before feasting.

Funeral customs in Tibet include leaving bodies in remote places for animals and birds to eat. In Sri Lanka, bodies are usually buried but some are cremated. In Theravada Buddhism, monks recite sacred texts for 12 days after a death.

■ Christianity

Christian marriages take place in front of God in church. The bride and groom promise to 'love and to cherish, for better for worse, for richer for poorer, in sickness and in health till death do us part'. The priest explains the importance of marriage in providing a stable and loving home for bringing up children.

Funeral services are held in church or at a crematorium. Many Christians are buried rather than cremated. A sermon explains Christian beliefs about life after death, and the good qualities of the deceased are described.

■ Hinduism

Grihasta (the second ashram, or stage of life) involves marriage and setting up a family unit. Wedding customs are elaborate and may take place in a temple or at home. The bride's father honours the groom, the mother and other women perform the consecration ceremony, the priest prays and the bride's sari and groom's scarf are tied together. The couple take seven steps around the sacred fire exchanging vows.

Vanaprashta (the third ashram) is retired life, when there is more time for spiritual things. The younger generation take over the running of the home, and social activities become more religious.

The final ashram is **sannyasa** or renunciation. Possessions and socialising are replaced with meditation and focusing on God. Few modern Hindus take this step.

The dead are usually cremated, with the mourners following the rituals to enable the soul to pass on to the next life rather than remaining as a ghost. The son performs the funeral rites and lights the pyre.

Objectives

Investigate marriage and funeral ceremonies.

links

Look back to page 106 to remind yourself of what is meant by rites of passage.

A A Christian wedding

B A Christian cemetery

C A Hindu bride

Chapter 5 Practices and belonging

■ Islam

A Muslim wedding is led by the imam and includes readings from the Qur'an and Hadith. There is a spoken and written contract and the groom gives his bride money or property (mahr). After a feast, the bride and groom go to their home and the next day family and friends attend the marriage celebration.

Muslims believe in the resurrection of the body after death and so bodies are buried with the right side facing Makkah. If possible, the body is dressed in the robes worn while on Hajj. Funeral prayers are said in the mosque and at the graveside.

■ Judaism

The bride and groom sign the ketubah (marriage contract). The groom stands under the canopy (chuppah) facing Jerusalem and the bride is brought by her mother to join him. The canopy symbolises their home. The bridegroom breaks a wine glass under his feet, recalling the destruction of the Temple in 70 CE, as those present shout 'Mazel tov' (good luck).

After death, burial usually takes place within a day. A short funeral service takes place; then the mourners go to the grave to fill it with earth. There follows a time of ritual mourning.

■ Sikhism

Sikhs make their wedding vows in front of the Guru Granth Sahib. The groom promises to protect the bride and she undertakes to fulfil her obligations. They hold the groom's scarf and walk clockwise around the Guru Granth Sahib while four hymns (lavan) are sung. Prayers are said, karah parshad eaten and presents are given to the couple.

At death, the body is washed, dressed in clean clothes and put in a coffin and cremated. A relative lights the funeral pyre, hymns are sung and prayers said. There are readings for the 10 days before the mourning period ends.

D *A Jewish bride and groom under a chuppah*

⊙⊙ links

Look back to page 64 to remind yourself of the destruction of the Temple in 70 CE.

Research activity

Using the internet or a library, find out more about the marriage and funeral ceremonies for the religions you are studying.

AQA Examiner's tip

Find out differences of practice within the faiths you are studying.

Discussion activity

With a partner, in a small group or as a class, discuss the idea that it is unwise to marry someone of a different faith. Make notes on the key points to use as examples in the examination.

Activities

1. Explain what happens at the marriage and funeral ceremonies for the religions you are studying, and their importance.

2. 'Marriage vows must never be broken.' Do you agree? Give reasons for your answer, showing that you have thought about more than one point of view.

Summary

You should now be able to explain what happens at the marriage and funeral ceremonies for the religions you are studying, and their importance.

5.8 Key festivals: Buddhism and Christianity

Festivals help a person feel a part of a faith. Each religion has a number of key festivals.

Buddhism

Wesak

Wesak (Vesak) is the most important religious festival for Buddhists because it celebrates the birth, enlightenment and death of the Buddha. Celebrated on the full moon in May, it is a very colourful festival as lights and decorations are put up in the home. In Thailand, lanterns are made out of paper and wood, and cards are sent to friends. Caged birds may be released, services held at the temple, and offerings of candles, flowers and food are presented to the monks. In some traditions, a statue of the Buddha is washed as it reminds Buddhists of the need to purify the heart and mind of greed, hatred and ignorance. Chinese Buddhists include dancing dragons as part of their celebrations, and gifts are given to charity.

> **Objectives**
> Know and understand the practices of key festivals in Buddhism and Christianity.

> **Key terms**
> **Wesak:** the festival commemorating the Buddha's birth, enlightenment and death.
> **Songkran:** Buddhist New Year celebration in Thailand.
> **Christmas:** festival to celebrate the birth of Jesus.
> **Easter:** festival to celebrate the resurrection of Jesus.

Case study

New Year celebrations

Songkran is the name of the Thai New Year celebrations, which are held annually between 13 and 15 April. It is a day when people drench each other in water fights, the water symbolising the washing away of everything bad. People carry water into the streets and use water guns to fire at each other, and some even use garden hoses. In Chiang Mai, images of the Buddha are paraded through the streets so people can throw water over them. Some decorate themselves using chalk. Traditionally, Songkran is a time to visit family, friends and neighbours. Many go to the Buddhist monasteries and give food to the monks. In northern Thailand, sand may be taken to the monasteries, where it is made into stupa-shaped piles and decorated with flags. New Year resolutions are made and the home is cleaned.

A Songkran festivities in Thailand

Christianity

Christmas

The festival of **Christmas**, held on 25 December, is when most Christians celebrate the birth of Jesus. The festivities last 12 days. Christian and non-Christian children look forward to receiving presents from Father Christmas. Shops, trees and homes are decorated with lights and nativity scenes. Families get together, cards are sent to friends and relatives and many parties take place. Special foods are prepared including Christmas cake, Christmas pudding and mince pies, and roast turkey is often eaten on Christmas Day. Special services are held where carols are sung, the nativity scene is acted out by the children and Midnight Mass takes place on Christmas Eve. It is seen as a time of 'peace and goodwill' and giving to charity as God gave the gift of his Son.

Easter

Easter is the most important Christian festival as it celebrates the resurrection of Jesus from the dead. The week leading up to Easter Day is known as Holy Week, and Christians remember the events that led to the sacrifice of Jesus on the cross. Jesus was crucified on 'Good Friday' and laid in the tomb. Special services are held and processions in the streets are led by a person carrying a wooden cross.

On Easter Sunday (Easter Day) the churches are filled with flowers and special hymns are sung celebrating the resurrection. Orthodox Christians walk around the church at midnight on the Saturday and then enter the darkened church with lighted candles or lamps. This symbolises entering the empty tomb. The priest announces 'Christ is risen!' and the congregation answers 'He is risen indeed'. Roman Catholics and Anglicans also have a Saturday-night vigil that begins in darkness, includes the lighting of a large Paschal candle to symbolise the risen Christ, and ends with Holy Communion. Many churches organise open-air sunrise services and share breakfast together, usually eating eggs, a symbol of new life.

B *Easter celebrates the death and resurrection of Jesus*

Discussion activity

With a partner, in a small group or as a class, discuss how festivals might help people understand the value of belonging to their religion. Make notes on the key points to use as examples in the examination.

Activities

1. Explain how Wesak and Songkran are celebrated and the reasons for these festivals.
2. Explain how Christians celebrate Christmas and Easter and the reasons for these festivals.
3. 'Festivals are just an excuse for a party.' What do you think? Explain your opinion.

Extension activity

Using the internet or a library, find out more about more about the key festivals of the religion(s) you are studying. Record your findings.

AQA Examiner's tip

You need to be able to explain that there are different customs in celebrating these festivals in different countries or different religious traditions.

Summary

You should now be able to explain what happens at two Buddhist and/or two Christian festivals, and their importance.

5.9 Key festivals: Hinduism and Islam

Hinduism

Diwali

Diwali (Divali) is celebrated by Hindus and Sikhs. Often known as the Festival of Lights, it symbolises the victory of good over evil. Lights are lit in the home and some are floated down the river. This symbolises the person's inner light (atman) outshining darkness and overcoming ignorance and obstacles, bringing an awareness of spiritual things. The lamps are small earthenware bowls filled with oil with a cotton wick, or small electric lights may be used. These are put inside and outside the houses, and Hindus remember the story from *The Ramayana* of Rama and Sita's welcome home after their victory over the evil king Ravana. Lakshmi (goddess of wealth) is thanked and worshipped, and people pray for blessings, happiness and a good year. The festival includes firecrackers, fireworks, giving and receiving presents and eating sweets, and is a great favourite with children. In Britain, Leicester has one of the biggest Diwali celebrations outside of India.

> **Objectives**
> Know and understand the practices of key festivals in Hinduism and Islam.

> **Key terms**
> **Diwali (Divali):** festival of lights (Hinduism, Sikhism).
> **Holi:** a joyous spring Hindu festival that is dedicated to Krishna.

> **links**
> See page 114 to find out how Sikhs celebrate Diwali.

Case study

Holi

Holi (the Festival of Colours) takes place in spring and celebrates new life and the triumph of good over evil. A bonfire is built and on the first day the effigy of the demoness Holika is burned on it. Food is partly roasted on the fire and served as prashad (holy food). Next day, children and adults enjoy throwing coloured powder or paint and water at each other. Distinctions between caste, class, age and gender are forgotten as everyone joins in the fun, and there are contests between men and women. There is dancing and singing, and children are carried around the fire. Some activities are associated with Krishna, who misbehaved with some milkmaids, and the story of him slaying the demoness Putana is sometimes told. Gifts of sweets and flowers are often given.

A *Holi powders*

Islam

Eid ul Fitr

Eid ul Fitr marks the end of the fast of Ramadan and lasts for three days as a thanksgiving for having the strength to complete the duty of fasting. Muslims pay Zakat-ul-Fitr, which provides enough money for the poor to celebrate the feast. The new moon signals the commencement of festivities. There is a sense of belonging to the ummah (Muslim brotherhood) because friends and relatives gather together, meeting in the homes and in the mosque for special prayers. Sermons include the importance of Eid and giving zakah, and prayers include asking for forgiveness and help for people everywhere.

> **Key terms**
> **Eid ul Fitr:** festival to mark the end of Ramadan.
> **Eid ul Adha:** festival of sacrifice celebrated at the end of the Hajj.

B *Special sweets may be given at Eid*

links
Look back to page 87 to see a picture of Muslims celebrating Eid ul Fitr.

Muslims wear their best or new clothes, there are parties (particularly for young people), presents are given and Eid cards are sent. Special foods are eaten, and many visit the cemeteries to show respect for their ancestors.

Eid ul Adha

Eid ul Adha (the Festival of Sacrifice) commemorates the story of how Ibrahim (Abraham) was willing to sacrifice his son Ishmael to Allah, but he heard a voice telling him to sacrifice a ram instead. It is celebrated by those on Hajj at Mina, on the way back to Makkah. An animal is killed and part of the meat is given to the poor.

Other Muslims also celebrate Eid ul Adha, and an animal (usually a sheep, but sometimes a camel, cow or goat) is brought for sacrifice. Festival prayers and a sermon occur in the mosque before the animal is slaughtered. The Qur'an gives instructions that the meat should be divided into three: one portion for the poor; one for relatives and neighbours; and one for oneself. A large portion is given to the poor so that they can join in the feast. It is a time of visiting friends and relatives, and is the most important Eid festival.

AQA Examiner's tip
Make sure that you can explain the reasons for the festivals as well as the fun activities that occur.

Activities

1. Explain how Diwali and Holi are celebrated and the reasons for the festivals.
2. Explain how Eid ul Fitr and Eid ul Adha are celebrated and the reasons for these festivals.
3. 'Feasting and wearing new clothes are the most important ways festivals are celebrated.' What do you think? Explain your opinion.

Discussion activity
With a partner, in a small group or as a class, discuss how festivals help young people understand the history and duties of their religion. Make notes on the opinions given, and the reasons for them.

Summary
You should now be able to explain what happens at two Hindu and/or two Muslim festivals, and their importance.

5.10 Key festivals: Judaism and Sikhism

Judaism

Rosh Hashanah

Rosh Hashanah is the Jewish New Year and there are three themes – creation, judgement and renewal. Apples are dipped in honey (for a sweet year), special bread is baked and pomegranates are eaten. A ram's horn (shofar) is blown to remind listeners of God's judgement, and there are special prayers and services in the synagogue. Cards are sent, and the day is treated like a Sabbath Day – a day of rest.

Yom Kippur

Yom Kippur is the Day of Atonement and the most solemn and holy of Jewish festivals. Jews spend 25 hours fasting and praying, asking God for forgiveness for their sins. It is the last of 10 days of repentance, which began with Rosh Hashanah, when people ask forgiveness of each other for any wrongs they may be guilty of. Much of Yom Kippur is spent in attending the synagogue, where the Ark is covered in white and some people wear a kittel (long white smock). Many Jews believe that God decides on a person's fate for the next year and seals his verdict at Yom Kippur. After sunset, the shofar is blown to bring an end to the fasting.

> **Objectives**
> Know and understand the practices of key festivals in Judaism and Sikhism.

> **Key terms**
> **Rosh Hashanah:** the Jewish New Year.
> **Yom Kippur:** the Day of Atonement – a day of fasting on the tenth day after Rosh Hashanah.
> **Pesach:** Passover festival celebrating the Exodus from Egypt.
> **Baisakhi:** festival that celebrates the formation of the Khalsa.

Case study: Pesach (Passover)

The festival of **Pesach** is very important as it remembers how God saved the Israelites from slavery in Egypt. During the night of the Tenth Plague, the angel of death passed over the land and all the first-born sons of the Egyptians were killed. None of the Israelites died. They had killed a lamb and put blood on the door of their house in the form of a cross in order to avoid the plague. This resulted in the Pharaoh allowing Moses and the Israelites to leave. Each year, a Passover Seder meal is held to celebrate their freedom. The items on the seder plate remind Jews of the story. The symbolic food includes matzah (unleavened) bread, bitter herbs (bitterness of slavery), salt water (tears of the slaves), charoset (almonds, apples, cinnamon and wine representing the mortar used with bricks), parsley or lettuce (symbolising spring and hope) dipped in the salt water, a roasted shank bone (representing the lamb) and a roasted egg (symbolising other sacrifices in the Temple).

A A rabbi blowing the shofar

> **Research activity**
> 1. Using the internet or a library, find out more about how Jews celebrate Pesach. Record your findings.

Sikhism

Diwali

Diwali is important to Sikhs because they remember the release from prison of Guru Hargobind and 52 other princes from Gwalior Fort. The Emperor had agreed to let Guru Hargobind go, and as many prisoners as could hold on to his cloak on the way out. The Guru attached 52 pieces of string to his cloak so everyone escaped. In addition to celebrating in similar style to Hindus, the Golden Temple at Amritsar is lit up by hundreds of lights.

> **links**
> Look back to page 112 to remind yourself about the Hindu festival, Diwali.

Chapter 5   Practices and belonging   115

Baisakhi

Baisakhi (or Vaisakhi) is the most important Sikh festival. It celebrates the Sikh New Year and Sikhs remember the anniversary of the founding of the Khalsa by Guru Gobind Singh in 1699, which Sikhs regard as the start of the Sikh community. The day begins with bathing, followed by devotions in the home. A service in the gurdwara reminds everyone of the historical events, and the cloth around the flagpole and the nishan sahib (flag) is renewed. New members are initiated into the Khalsa.

B *Sikh women celebrate Baisakhi*

Discussion activity

With a partner, in a small group or as a class, discuss what you think are the main reasons for having religious festivals for members of the faith. Make a list of words that describe these ideas, e.g. belonging.

Activities

1. Explain how Pesach, Rosh Hashanah and Yom Kippur are celebrated and the reasons for these festivals.

2. Explain how Sikhs celebrate Diwali and Baisakhi, and the reasons for these festivals.

3. 'Religious people of all faiths should share in each other's festivals.' Do you agree? Give reasons for your answer, showing that you have thought about more than one point of view.

Summary

You should now be able to explain what happens at three Jewish and/or two Sikh festivals, and their importance.

Research activity

2. Using the internet or a library, find out more about how Sikhs celebrate Diwali or Baisakhi. Record your findings.

links

For more details on the origins of Baisakhi and the actions of Guru Gobind Singh, see page 90.

AQA Examiner's tip

Make sure that you can explain why these festivals are regarded as key festivals for the religions you have chosen.

Assessment guidance

5

Practices and belonging – summary

With reference to at least **two** of the religions you have studied, for the examination you should now be able to:

- ✔ show awareness of the importance and value of religious practices and belonging to a religion
- ✔ explain the behaviour codes, the need to follow them and the attitudes to those who do not
- ✔ explain and evaluate religious duties
- ✔ explain dietary laws and the challenges they present to believers living in a multicultural society
- ✔ explain and evaluate the importance of prayer and meditation
- ✔ explain the importance and value of rites of passage
- ✔ give details of the key festivals and explain their importance and value.

Sample answer

1 Write an answer to the following examination question:

'Belonging to a religion is really valuable.'

Do you agree? Give reasons for your answer, showing that you have thought about more than one point of view. Refer to religious arguments in your answer.
(6 marks)

2 Read the following sample answer:

> Belonging to a religion is valuable because you can really feel part of something that is important throughout the world. You could travel to many other countries and find members of the same religion there and locally it opens up an opportunity to have lots of friends who think like you do. You feel that you are part of a community and are valued and you have someone to go to, to talk through problems and get advice. This applies not only to the religious leaders, but also to the sacred writings, which may help in a situation you find yourself in. Socially as well you get friends who also belong to the religion to mix with. Belonging to a faith also enables you to really get involved in the festivals and celebrations. Although others may celebrate the festivals, it hasn't got the same meaning if you are not a member of the religion. So I agree with the statement that belonging to a religion is really valuable.

3 With a partner, discuss the sample answer. Do you think that there are other things that the student could have included in the answer?

4 What mark would you give this answer out of 6? (Look at the mark scheme in the Introduction on page 7 (A02) before you attempt this.) What are the reasons for the mark you have given?

AQA Examination-style questions

1 Look at the photographs and answer the following questions.

   (a) Give an example of a religious duty. *(1 mark)*

   AQA Examiner's tip: If the command word is 'Give', you do not have to give an explanation. An answer like 'pray' would be sufficient to get 1 mark.

   (b) Choose an example from the behaviour codes for **each** of the **two** religions you have studied and explain what they mean. *(4 marks)*

   AQA Examiner's tip: If you choose two examples from one religion, you will only gain a maximum of 2 marks.

   (c) 'Religious dietary laws are still important.' What do you think? Explain your opinion. *(3 marks)*

   AQA Examiner's tip: Use examples from the two religions you are studying to support your arguments.

   (d) Explain the importance of funeral ceremonies. *(4 marks)*

   AQA Examiner's tip: Don't just describe what happens in funeral ceremonies, but explain the importance to family and friends.

   (e) 'Festivals should always be joyful occasions.'
   Do you agree? Give reasons for your answer, showing that you have thought about more than one point of view. Refer to religious arguments in your answer. *(6 marks)*

   AQA Examiner's tip: Remember that when you are given a statement and asked 'do you agree?' you must show what you think and the reasons why other people might take a different view. If your answer is one sided, you can only achieve a maximum of 4 marks. If you make no comment about religious belief or practice, you will achieve no more than 3 marks.

6 Religious authority

6.1 Introduction: authority and leadership

What is authority?

The Concise Oxford Dictionary defines **authority** as (1) 'the power or right to enforce obedience'.

Discussion activity

1. a With a partner, spend two minutes compiling a list of people who have 'the power or right to enforce obedience' over you.
   b Compare your list with the list of another pair. Discuss similarities and differences between the two lists.

It is likely that many of you included the police and armed forces in your list. They clearly do have authority, but in carrying out their role they are subject to the authority of their 'higher ranked' officers who in turn, like all of us, are ultimately subject to the authority of the monarch and parliament. At home, you are likely to be under the authority of a parent or parents. Their authority over you is part of their duty to help you grow into a responsible member of society.

Objectives

Investigate the meanings of authority and leadership.

Evaluate qualities of leadership.

Key terms

Authority: the power exercised by someone who advises or has leadership over others.

Leadership: taking the role of directing others in tasks or activities.

A Figures of authority

B

However, the dictionary definition goes on to mention (2) 'an influence exerted on opinion because of recognised knowledge or expertise; such an influence expressed in a book, quotation, etc.', and (3) 'a person whose opinion is accepted, especially an expert in a subject'.

This gives a more complete picture of what authority is.

Leadership

Some people seem to be born leaders, whilst others prefer to take direction from a leader. From your teaching group, you could probably name some leaders and some who prefer to be directed. Neither one is better than the other, and both are necessary. People who have authority usually take a **leadership** role. However, in order to earn the respect of those whom they are leading, they have to possess certain qualities.

> **Discussion activity**
>
> 2 a With a partner, discuss and make a list of the qualities you would expect a good leader to possess.
> b Reduce your list to the **five** qualities you think are the most important and write them down in order of importance.
> c Compare your most important quality with the ones chosen by other groups.

If a leader possesses good qualities, they are likely to find their leadership role easier – those they are leading will be happy to be led by them and it is more likely that whatever they are doing will be successful. They need to be able to motivate their team to complete the task that is being set, preferably in ways that are appreciated by the different individuals making up the team. Some members of the team may need to be told, whereas others may respond better to being asked. What may be seen as a weakness to some may be a strength to others.

> **Activities**
>
> 2 Most political leaders are elected by the people or party they lead. Do you think this is the best way? Explain why.
>
> 3 Other leaders may be chosen by just one person or a small number of people. Think of some examples and decide what are the benefits and drawbacks of this way of choosing.

> **Summary**
>
> You should now understand authority and leadership and be able to decide what makes someone a good or a poor leader.

> **Activity**
>
> 1 a Explain how the first dictionary definition quoted differs from the second and third.
> b Which of the definitions do you find most useful? Explain why.

> **AQA Examiner's tip**
>
> If writing about leadership, make sure that you use examples to support what you are writing.

C The England football coach is chosen by just a few people

6.2 Leadership of religion

Leadership structures

Most organisations have a leadership structure in the shape of a triangle. Right at the top is the overall leader. Below the overall leader is usually a small team of senior managers who report to the overall leader. They have managers below them until eventually, at the bottom, there are a large number of ordinary people with no leadership role. However, whilst leadership comes from the top downwards, it is quite possible for ideas to come from the bottom upwards.

Activity

1.
   a. Using around 10–12 lines of your paper, draw an upright triangle.
   b. Try to fit the structure of your school into your triangle with the head teacher at the top. Include the pupils.
   c. Does your school structure fit this pattern?

The leadership structure of some religions or denominations is very similar. Take, for example, the Roman Catholic Church. At the top is the Pope, God's representative on earth. Below the Pope are cardinals, from whom the next Pope will be elected, archbishops, bishops, priests and individual Roman Catholics. The lower down the triangle you go, the larger the group of people becomes. However, in the case of the Roman Catholic Church, the Pope's word is believed to express the will of God, and Roman Catholics believe that he cannot be wrong on religious or ethical matters.

Nevertheless, the leaders of any organisation, including a religion, have to keep in mind the thoughts and feelings of people below them, listen to their opinions and, if necessary, allow them to influence future policy and developments.

Case study: The Dalai Lama

Sometimes, the choice of a leader is a little unusual. This was so with the leader of Tibetan Buddhists who is known by the title 'The Dalai Lama'. He was born in July 1935 and his parents named him Lhamo Dhondub (alternative spelling: Dhondrub). When he was two years old, Buddhist officials recognised him as the reincarnation of the 13 previous Dalai Lamas, and so at the age of four, Lhamo Dhondub was enthroned as the fourteenth Dalai Lama, taking the new name of Tenzin Gyatso. Tibetan Buddhists recognise him not only as a spiritual leader but also as a political leader. He became head of state in 1950 against the background of a Chinese invasion which took control of Tibet in 1951. In 1959, he fled Tibet and settled in India, which is still his home.

Objectives

Understand leadership structures.

Relate leadership structures to religious leadership where appropriate.

Consider the qualities that religious leaders need.

AQA Examiner's tip

Even though the Roman Catholic Church is only one denomination of Christianity, you can use it to give an example of religious leadership structure.

A St Peter – the first Pope

links

Look back to pages 70 and 124 for more information about the Dalai Lama.

The role of leadership

In theory, the people leading religions could introduce new interpretations of holy books or, for example, initiate changes in worship and alter teachings on ethical issues. However, they are well advised to go back to the historical roots of their faith before making a decision. In Judaism, for example, tradition is very important. Ultra Orthodox Jews will not entertain any thought of making changes from the way things have always been done unless there is a very compelling reason to do so. Muslims will refer to the unchanging teachings from the Qur'an for advice, and Sikhs believe that their holy book, the Guru Granth Sahib, is their earthly leader. For this reason, it is never changed.

Buddhism and especially Hinduism do not have a rigid structure. They could be considered to be more individual faiths. They do, however, have people who can offer advice and assistance on religious matters and lead meditation or worship.

B *A Jewish rabbi writing in a scroll*

Activity

2 'A human leader is a better leader than an old book.' What do you think? Explain your opinion.

Authority for religious leadership

Believers expect to know where the authority of their religious leaders comes from. All theistic religions believe that God is the divine leader and human leaders have to reflect his wishes. But if humans claim they have God's authority to justify leadership positions, believers have to trust that their leaders do have this authority. In most denominations of Christianity, priests are **ordained** to give them authority from God. This allows them to perform the functions of a priest, including distributing bread and wine in Holy Communion (Mass in the Roman Catholic Church) and delivering absolution to forgive sins.

Imams in Islam are chosen by the community, who look for wisdom and knowledge of the faith and the Qur'an. This allows them to give good advice on matters of faith.

Key terms

Ordained: appointed as a minister of the Christian Church.

links

See page 130 for more information about imams.

Discussion activity

With a partner, suggest the **six** qualities you would most expect a religious leader to have. Write them down and explain why you think they are important.

Summary

You should now know about and understand leadership structures and the human leadership of various religions, including the source of their authority. You will also have considered the qualities that religious leaders need.

6.3 Holy books and leadership

The importance of holy books

All religions have holy books and treat them with respect because the information they contain is considered to be important. They contain teachings from their founders or other great characters in the religion's history. Theistic religions believe that God has had some part in the writing of holy books. If this belief is true, it gives them greater authority and importance.

As the words are written down, it is often believed that they are more likely to be accurate than if they were spoken. The earliest copies in existence can be checked if there is any dispute about accuracy. However, Sikhism is the only religion that claims that the original copy of its holy book, the Adi Granth, is still in existence.

Discussion activities

1. Why do you think that a written record is more likely to be accurate than a spoken one?

2. If the Guru Granth Sahib is the only holy book where the original exists (the Adi Granth), does this mean it is the only one we can trust? Discuss this with a partner and give reasons for your answer.

The Qur'an

Muslims believe that in their holy book, the Qur'an, are the actual words of Allah as given to the prophet Muhammad and later written down with complete accuracy in Arabic. Every Arabic Qur'an is written using identical words, and the language is not updated. The Qur'an is translated into other languages, but it is recognised that, in doing so, errors occur because some Arabic words do not translate accurately –

Objectives

Understand that religions place great importance on their holy books.

Analyse and evaluate the authority given to holy books.

Activity

1. 'The only leader a religion needs is their holy book.' Do you agree? Give reasons for your answer, showing that you have thought about more than one point of view.

AQA Examiner's tip

The Qur'an can also be spelt Koran, although Qur'an is the spelling preferred by Muslims and this is what you should use in the examination.

A The Qur'an

there may not be a corresponding word in the other language. Thus, copies of the Qur'an in any language except Arabic are considered less important because they are not completely accurate. If Muslims want an answer to any religious or ethical problem, they will consult the Qur'an, and possibly ask an imam (a Muslim leader) to interpret it for them.

The Guru Granth Sahib

Sikhs also treat their holy book, the Adi Granth, with respect. It is often referred to as the Guru Granth Sahib – Guru meaning teacher and Sahib being a term of respect meaning 'sir' or 'lord'. It is considered the supreme spiritual authority and the unchanging leader of the Sikh religion, and has taken over from human Gurus. It is treated with great respect, as a human Guru would be, and even 'put to bed' at night.

links

See page 135 to find more about the respect shown to the Guru Granth Sahib.

B *The room in which the Guru Granth Sahib is put to bed*

Holy books in other faiths

Other faiths respect their own holy books greatly, and most followers use them for advice and guidance. They tend not to give them such a prominent leadership role though. However, religious leaders will use their holy books to inform them of the teachings of their faith and pass these teachings and their interpretations of them on to believers. They consult them when answering questions about religious or moral issues.

links

Read the rest of this chapter to find out more about the holy books and scriptures in all six religions covered in this book.

Activities

2. Write down some reasons why holy books are treated with great respect.

3. Explain why holy books are believed to have authority.

Summary

You should now know how holy books are respected and understand why believers accept their importance as a source of authority.

6.4 Authority in Buddhism

Most Buddhists do not acknowledge the existence of a living leader of their faith. Nor do they have priests as such, although their meditation in a vihara (shrine) will be led by a respected member of the Buddhist community, often a monk. The Buddhist scriptures are a good source of advice and teaching, although the teachings of the Buddha, Siddattha Gotama, were not written down until 400 years after his death. There is no doubt that some Buddhists have authority to lead, but as there is no belief in God in Buddhism the authority comes from within, achieved through meditation and spiritual discipline.

The Dalai Lama

The most easily recognisable Buddhist leader is the Dalai Lama. However, he is primarily the spiritual leader of Tibetan Buddhism, which is a branch of Mahayana Buddhism. Other Buddhists, whilst recognising him as an important man, do not accept him as their leader. Tibetan Buddhists believe he is a rebirth of the compassionate Buddha Chenrezig, which gives him great authority.

Research activity

1. Using the internet or a library, find out more about the present Dalai Lama and especially his role as a political leader that has resulted in his exile.

The sangha: the order of monks

The sangha is the third refuge for Buddhists (the first two are the Buddha and the dhamma– teachings). In Theravada Buddhism, being a monk, part of the sangha, is essential to reach enlightenment. In Mahayana Buddhism, it is not essential but the sangha is valued. Lay Buddhists (Buddhists who are not monks) provide food for monks in order to earn good kamma (karma) by sharing. In return, the monks provide a good example of living by following at least five more precepts in addition to the five that all Buddhists follow:

1. Not eating at the wrong time.
2. No dancing, singing or music.
3. No use of garlands, perfume or jewellery.
4. No use of high seats to increase perceptions of their importance.
5. Not accepting gold or silver.

Although monks don't have a leadership role or any more authority than lay Buddhists, they may lead meditation in the vihara and give instruction on how to meditate. Their knowledge of Buddhism will provide valuable assistance for lay Buddhists. However, lay Buddhists can perform the same role.

Discussion activity

With a partner, in a small group or as a whole class, discuss whether you think a monk is a good person to give advice, and why.

Objectives

Understand the way leadership works in Buddhism.

Evaluate the effectiveness of this leadership.

links

Look back to page 120 for information about how the Dalai Lama was chosen, and page 70 for more information about him.

A The Dalai Lama

links

Look back to page 97 to remind yourself of the Five Moral Precepts.

AQA Examiner's tip

You are not expected to know about the difference between Theravada and Mahayana Buddhism, but examples from either tradition of their practices and beliefs will help you answer questions.

B A Theravadan monk in a shrine room

The Tripitaka: the scriptures

For Theravadan Buddhists, the most important scriptures are the Tripitaka, also known as 'The Three Baskets'. They contain teachings of the Buddha together with the rules for the sangha. The Three Baskets (pitaka) are:

1. The **Vinaya Pitaka**, containing the Four Noble Truths, the Noble Eightfold Path, and the rules for the sangha.
2. The **Sutta Pitaka**, containing dialogues involving the teachings of the Buddha and stories of his life.
3. The **Abhidamma Pitaka**, containing explanations of the teachings in the Sutta Pitaka.

Mahayana Buddhists also acknowledge the importance of the Tripitaka, but have other scriptures as well.

The scriptures are used to provide teachings and advice and also in meditation in mantras (words or phrases repeated to aid concentration whilst meditating).

Summary
You should now know about different sources of authority in Buddhism and have thought about their importance.

Research activity
2. Using the internet or a library, try to find examples of Buddhist scriptures and read a short passage from them.

Activities
1. 'The Buddha's teaching in the Tripitaka cannot be accurate because it was written down so long after his death.' What do you think? Explain your opinion.
2. Which do you think is the most important leader for Buddhists?
   - The Dalai Lama
   - The sangha
   - The Tripitaka

   Explain your opinion.

6.5 Authority in Christianity

Christianity is a very complex religion, which is reflected in the fact that it is split into three main groups, known as denominations. These groups, Roman Catholic, Protestant (itself split into many other denominations) and Eastern Orthodox, have different ideas about leadership and authority.

In view of the fact that the Christian Church in Britain is mainly Roman Catholic and Church of England (Protestant), these two denominations will be our main focus.

The Roman Catholic Church

As you learnt earlier, the leader of the Roman Catholic Church is the Pope. He is thought to have direct authority from God, following in a line of descent from St Peter, one of Jesus' disciples who became the first Pope. The Pope is elected after much prayer by the cardinals, who believe they are helping to make God's choice. He will remain as Pope until he dies, at which time the next Pope will be elected in the same way. Roman Catholics believe that because he is God's choice, God leads and inspires him, so that whenever he speaks about religious or ethical matters he is correct. This gives him enormous authority because all individual Roman Catholics are supposed to do and think as he tells them.

A *The Vatican in Rome – centre of the Roman Catholic Church*

Objectives

Understand different leadership structures and sources of authority in Christianity.

Evaluate the effectiveness of this leadership.

∞ links

Look back to page 120 to remind yourself about the Pope and the structure of the Roman Catholic Church.

AQA Examiner's tip

Do not use the phrase 'Roman Catholics and Christians' to show denominational differences. Roman Catholics *are* Christians.

Discussion activity

With a partner, discuss whether you feel it is good that one person can have such authority over people as the Pope does. Give reasons for your answer, showing that you have thought about more than one point of view.

The Church of England

The Church of England began in 1534 when King Henry VIII, previously a loyal Roman Catholic, was declared 'the only supreme head of the Church of England' by the English parliament. Today, the monarch is still supreme head of the Church of England – the established Church in Britain. Effectively, the Archbishop of Canterbury (chosen by the Prime Minister) is the head of the Church, supported by the Archbishop of York and many other bishops, each in charge of a diocese (a region containing a cathedral whose churches are governed by the bishop in charge of the cathedral). They have a 'government' called the General Synod, which meets to debate and approve policy. Othersmaller Protestant denominations (e.g. the Baptist Church, Methodist and United Reformed) have their own simple structures of leadership. The main source of authority for a Protestant church is the holy book – the Bible.

The Bible

The Bible is very important for Christians. They believe that the many writers of the Bible were inspired by God in their writing, which gives it a special authority. It contains the history and teachings of the Israelites (forefathers of present-day Jews), including the Ten Commandments, the life, work and teachings of Jesus, and the early days of the Christian Church with a focus on St Paul. Protestant Christians believe that the Bible is the ultimate authority for Christians and look to it for advice and guidance. Roman Catholics also acknowledge its importance but place it second to the Pope on religious and ethical issues. However, the Pope uses it to determine Roman Catholic beliefs, practice and policy.

B *The Archbishop of Canterbury*

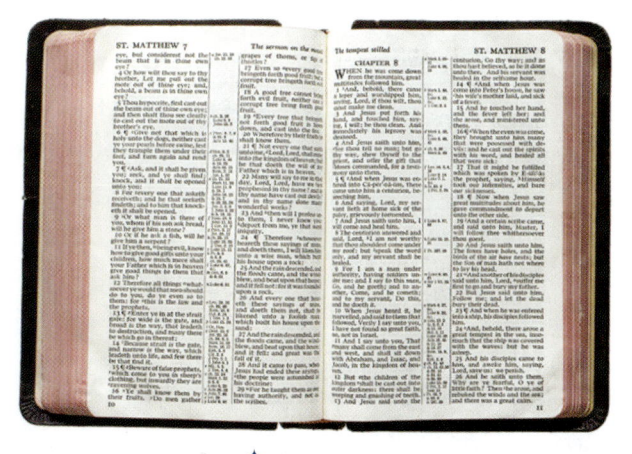

C *The Bible*

Activities

1. a. Explain the differences and similarities in leadership and authority between the Roman Catholic Church and the Church of England.
   b. In your opinion, are these differences important? Give reasons for your answer.

2. 'The Bible is more likely to be correct than any person.' What do you think? Explain your opinion.

Research activity

Using the internet or a library, try to find examples of Christian scriptures and read a short passage from them.

Summary

You should now know about different sources of authority in Christianity and have thought about their importance.

6.6 Authority in Hinduism

Because of the diversity in Hindu belief and practice, there is no overall structure of authority within Hinduism. Historically, the caste system (rigid social class system) included the Brahmin or priestly class who performed priestly functions. Despite the fact that the caste system is now illegal in India, the priestly class of Brahmins still exists. Their authority comes from their high caste and also from their knowledge of the law and practices of Hinduism.

Hindu leadership in Britain

Hindus worship in a mandir. Each mandir (or group of mandirs) is run by a committee of senior Hindus who are respected for their experience and wisdom. A mandir will have at least one pandit or priest who is responsible for offering advice on individual daily worship (puja). They accept offerings to place in front of the Hindu gods (murtis) and lead group worship.

A *Murtis in a mandir (Hindu temple)*

Pandits also have responsibility for giving advice on family and ethical matters and preparing horoscopes, especially for a newborn baby or connected with a marriage – a ceremony they will lead. Their authority comes from their knowledge of Hinduism, often derived from being a scholar of Sanskrit – the ancient language of Hinduism. Whilst they do not have to be from the Brahmin caste, many are.

Objectives

Understand the leadership and sources of authority in Hinduism.

Evaluate the effectiveness of this leadership.

Discussion activity

Priests were near the top of the caste system in India.

With a partner, in a small group or as a whole class, discuss whether you think that priests should be near the top of any social class system. Give reasons for your answer, showing that you have thought about more than one point of view.

AQA Examiner's tip

Always try to use the correct technical term: for example, in Hinduism, use mandir instead of temple and pandit instead of priest.

B *Hindu scriptures with puja offerings*

> **Key terms**
>
> **Shruti (Srti, Sruti):** the oldest and most sacred Hindu scriptures, the Vedas, which were heard and revealed to the wise.
>
> **Smriti:** Hindu scriptures which were remembered through human tradition and so, in theory, rank below Shruti.

Hindu scriptures

The Hindu scriptures are extremely old, most of them more than 2000 years old. They are divided into two sections: **Shruti** and **Smriti**.

Shruti scriptures

The Shruti scriptures ('that which is heard') are the oldest ones, which were revealed by God to ancient seers. They are 'closed' and therefore cannot be changed or added to. Originally, they were passed by word of mouth by priests, and because they were considered to be so important they were remembered. Even after they had been written down they were still passed on orally with great accuracy. They consist of the Vedas (knowledge), the oldest being the Rig Veda, and contain hymns, verses and texts explaining religious concepts such as meditation, sacrifice and the universe. Within the Shruti scriptures are also the Upanishads, which are believed to reveal hidden truths.

Smriti scriptures

The Smriti scriptures ('that which is remembered') are not as old as the Shruti scriptures and are not considered to have such great authority. They are considered 'open' so can be added to by Hindu scholars and poets if required. The most well-known Smriti scriptures are the epic poems called *The Mahabharata* and *The Ramayana*. They both focus on the stories of the deeds of the gods. The Smriti scriptures also include, in addition to several other ancient manuscripts, the Laws of Manu, which give ethical advice to Hindus and the rules of priesthood.

Conclusion

As Hinduism is a religion focused on the individual, they do not have the structure that some other religions have. However, they have priests called pandits whose learning and wisdom give them authority. They take their priestly rules from the Laws of Manu – one of the Smriti scriptures which reinforces their authority.

> **Research activity**
>
> Using the internet or a library, try to find examples of Hindu scriptures and read a short passage from them.

> **Activities**
>
> 1. Explain the difference between Shruti and Smriti scriptures.
>
> 2. 'It is difficult to claim authority from scriptures that are over 2000 years old.' What do you think? Explain your opinion.

> **Summary**
>
> You should now know about different sources of authority in Hinduism and have thought about their importance.

6.7 Authority in Islam

The ultimate authority in Islam is Allah. It is Allah who gave Muslims their holy book, the Qur'an, and so it is from the Qur'an that all Muslims get advice and teachings on their religion in the belief that it is Allah's Word. Human leaders also take their authority from Allah via the Qur'an.

Human leadership

Islam is very much a way of life centred on Allah. Many Islamic countries are ruled by Muslims in accordance with their Islamic faith. The law and their legal system are Islamic, and so some Muslims in positions of power have great influence, which they exercise on behalf of Allah.

Britain is not like this. Muslims in Britain have a 'parliament' but it debates matters of faith and living and has no power to pass laws. Its remit is to work towards creating a caring, informed and morally upright Muslim community in Britain. It has no official links to the British government.

At a community level, every mosque (place of worship) has an imam to lead prayers, preach a sermon every Friday lunchtime, look after the pastoral needs of the community and lead ceremonies. An imam is selected by the community. In order to be an imam, a Muslim must have an in-depth knowledge of Islam and be respected by their community. Their authority is from their learning and their practice of their faith – both of which are required by Allah.

A *An imam leading prayers*

> **Objectives**
>
> Understand leadership and sources of authority in Islam.
>
> Evaluate the effectiveness of this leadership.

> **Discussion activity**
>
> Imams are respected for their learning and way of life.
>
> With a partner, in a small group or as a whole class, discuss what qualities you think a Muslim religious leader must possess. Explain your opinion.

> **Activity**
>
> 1. Do you think religious groups should have the authority to set up parliaments that cannot pass laws? Give reasons for your opinion.

> **Research activity**
>
> 1. Using the internet or a library, find out more about a day in the life of an imam.

Written authority

The Qur'an is the main Islamic source of authority, containing what Muslims believe to be the Word of Allah given to the prophet Muhammad by the angel Jibril. The Hadith are complementary to the Qur'an; in some scholars' eyes they clarify some parts of the Qur'an. They are the oral tradition that relate to the words and deeds of Muhammad. This is where information about **Sunnah**, the Islamic way of life, is obtained. The Sunnah is the way of the prophet – the religious actions that were instituted by the prophet Muhammad. These were passed on through word of mouth by Muhammad's followers. Muslims are keen to follow the Sunnah out of respect to Muhammad whose example they wish to follow.

The Qur'an and Sunnah inform Islamic **Shari'ah**. This is a religious law that governs areas such as banking, business, contracts, family and social issues. Although Muslims in Britain are subject to British law and the British legal system, Shari'ah arbitration tribunals are permitted as an alternative way of resolving commercial, civil and matrimonial disputes to the satisfaction of both sides.

Key terms

Sunnah: teachings and example of Muhammad which Muslims must follow.

Shari'ah: Islamic law based directly on the Qur'an and Sunnah.

links

Look back to page 122 for more information about the Qur'an.

Case study: The Muslim Arbitration Tribunal

Sheikh Faiz-ul-Aqtab Siddiqi is chairman of the governing council of the Muslim Arbitration Tribunal based in Nuneaton, Warwickshire. One of its roles is to oversee Shari'ah Courts that have been set up in cities with high Muslim populations such as Birmingham, London, Bradford and Manchester. Both parties to a dispute have to agree to accept the finding of the court which is legally binding. The courts arbitrate on matters such as divorce and financial disputes, but have also heard cases of domestic violence. Mr Siddiqi expects these courts to arbitrate on more 'smaller criminal cases' in the future.

AQA Examiner's tip

In the examination, even if you are not a Muslim, you can refer to God as Allah when writing about Islam.

Activities

2. Explain how Muslims believe that Allah shows his authority through people and holy books.

3. In your opinion, what are the advantages of Muslims resolving disputes using Shari'ah?

Research activity

2. Find out more about the Muslim Arbitration Tribunal at www.matribunal.com.

Summary

You should now know about different sources of authority in Islam and have thought about their importance.

6.8 Authority in Judaism

Judaism may be divided into three distinct groups:

1. Ultra Orthodox
2. Orthodox
3. Reform

Part of the difference between them is in how strictly they interpret the authority of the Jewish law as outlined in the Torah (the first five books of the Bible). This is evident in their daily life as well as in their worship.

Holy books

The written words in the Torah are of great importance to Jews. In addition to accounts of ancient Jewish history, including the story of the creation of the universe, the Torah contains 613 laws or mitzvot, including the Ten Commandments. These laws range from telling Jews not to murder (Exodus 20:13) to laws on observing Shabbat (Leviticus 23:3) and freeing servants (Deuteronomy 15:12). All Jews consider them important because they were given to them by Moses after he had received them from God. They are therefore Divine Law. Ultra Orthodox Jews try to keep each of the 613 laws just as they are written, whilst Reform Jews try to keep the spirit of the law, recognising that some may be impractical to obey literally in the modern world. Orthodox Jews fall somewhere in between the other two groups. A good example of this is how they observe the Shabbat laws.

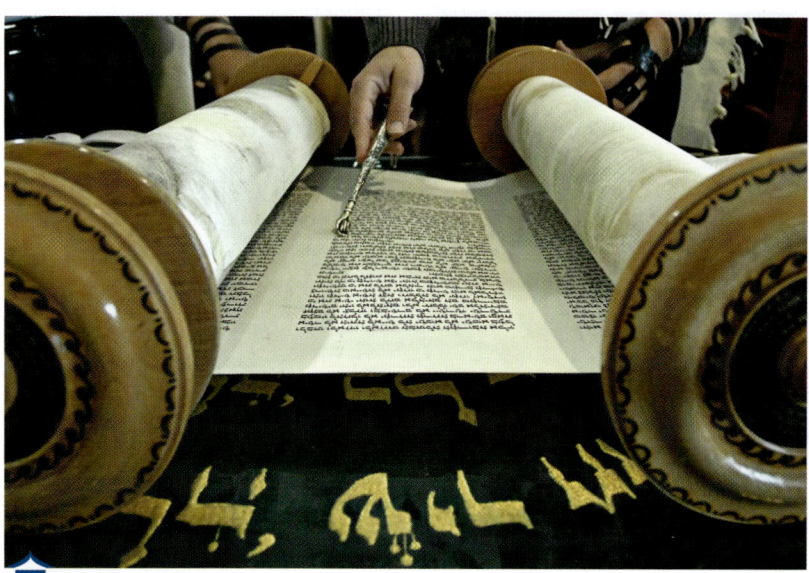

A *A Torah scroll*

Objectives

Understand leadership and sources of authority in Judaism.

Evaluate the effectiveness of this leadership.

AQA Examiner's tip

Whilst you don't need to distinguish between the three groups of Jews in the examination, knowing some differences may help your understanding.

Links

Look back to page 46 to remind yourself of how Jews observe Shabbat, and to page 100 for more on mitzvot.

Research activity

Have a look at the laws of Kashrut (clean and unclean food) in Leviticus 11:1–47 as an example of what the laws are like.

Activity

1. Do you think it is best to follow the Ultra Orthodox view and follow every letter of the law, or the Reform view that the spirit of the law is more important? Give reasons for your answer. It may help to use what you have learnt previously about observance of Shabbat.

The rest of the Jewish scriptures (which, like the Torah, are contained in the Old Testament in the Bible) are divided into the Nevi'im (prophecy inspired by God) and Ketuvim (other holy writings).

Many of the laws in the Torah are quite brief, so by around 200 CE an oral tradition had developed that interpreted the 613 mitzvot and gave advice on how best to keep them. These interpretations were collected and written down in what is called the Mishnah. Between 200 CE and around 500 CE, many learned Jews discussed the Mishnah and gave further advice that ended up combined with the Mishnah in the Talmud. This is now the main authority on the Law of Moses and is regularly consulted.

Key terms

Talmud: the written version of the oral instructions (Mishnah) passed down from Moses along with the commentary on them (Gemara).

Bet Din: Jewish religious court made up of rabbis.

Discussion activity

'The Mishnah has six divisions. One of them is devoted specifically to women's issues, none specifically to men's issues.' Think about this statement and discuss with a partner why this might be. Be prepared to share your ideas with the class.

links

Look back to page 103 to remind yourself of what is meant by kosher, or you can look it up in the Glossary at the back of this book.

Human leaders

Israel, the only Jewish state in the world, has a secular government but it is influenced by Judaism as the main religion of Israel.

In Britain, the most prominent Jewish leaders are the rabbis, who serve their community through their position in the synagogue. Rabbis, who may be female in Reform Judaism, are experts on the Law of Moses and may even have a specialist interest. The **Bet Din** is a group of rabbis appointed to judge on various matters within the Jewish community, including kosher certification for which they must have extensive knowledge. In the synagogue, rabbis will lead Shabbat prayers and perhaps preach the sermon. They also have a pastoral role in the community, advising Jews about living a good Jewish life keeping the Law of Moses and supporting them in this.

B A rabbi reading

Activities

2. Explain how Jews believe that God exercises his authority on earth.

3. If you were able to ask a rabbi for one piece of advice about living a Jewish life, what would it be? Be prepared to answer somebody else's question and for them to answer yours.

Summary

You should now know about different sources of authority in Judaism and have thought about their importance.

6.9 Authority in Sikhism

Sikhs believe in one eternal God who created and sustains the earth. He is often referred to as Waheguru (Wonderful Lord). The Mool Mantar, the statement of belief at the beginning of the Guru Granth Sahib, says: 'God can be known by the Guru's grace.'

Guru means 'teacher', and between 1499 and 1708 there were Ten Gurus who had God's authority to lead people to God.

The Ten Gurus

The first of the Ten Gurus was Guru Nanak. In around 1499, he had a spiritual experience whilst bathing in the river Bain. He disappeared for three days and when he re-emerged he claimed to have had visions that gave him the authority to found the new religion of Sikhism, which grew out of Hinduism and Islam. Before he died, he passed his God-given authority to Guru Angad, whom he had chosen to succeed him. This succession and passing of authority like a flame from one candle to another lasted until the tenth Guru, Guru Gobind Rai (Singh). Each Guru (apart perhaps from Guru Har Krishan, the eighth Guru who died at the age of 8) developed and advanced the faith. Guru Gobind Rai declared himself as the last human Guru in favour of the Adi Granth. This became the permanent Guru and is known as the Guru Granth Sahib – the holy book of Sikhism.

> **Objectives**
> Understand leadership and sources of authority in Sikhism.
> Evaluate the effectiveness of this leadership.

> **Key terms**
> **Guru:** a Sikh religious teacher.

> **Research activity**
> Using the internet or a library, research the Mool Mantar and find out what else it says about God.

> **Discussion activity**
>
> 1. a With a partner, make a list of the advantages and disadvantages of a Guru choosing their successor.
>   b What other ways could they have used to choose a leader?

A Guru Nanak

B An empty prayer hall. The Guru Granth Sahib will be placed on the platform (takht).

The Guru Granth Sahib

The Guru Granth Sahib is thus believed to have the authority of God, just like all the other Ten Gurus. It contains the teachings of Guru Nanak and some of the other Gurus, collected together by Guru Arjan, the fifth Guru. It is the central feature in all gurdwaras, where it is shown great respect – evidence of its authority as the word of the Gurus inspired by God.

Before Sikhs walk into the prayer room, they wash themselves and cover their head. They then approach the Guru Granth Sahib and bow towards it. After leaving a small offering of money, they will walk to a space on the carpet without turning their back towards the Guru Granth Sahib and sit down without their feet pointing directly towards it. They will then listen in silence while it is read by a granthi, an official who also has the authority to lead worship in the gurdwara. A selection of hymns from the Guru Granth Sahib has been gathered together in the small book known as the Gutka and is used in worship.

links

Look back to page 123 for more about the Guru Granth Sahib.

AQA Examiner's tip

In the examination, the holy book will be called the Guru Granth Sahib. However, if you refer to it as the Adi Granth, you will not lose marks.

C *The Guru Granth Sahib being read aloud*

Activities

1. a Note down all the ways the Guru Granth Sahib is shown respect. (Refer to pages 23 and 48 also.)
   b Why do you think such respect is shown towards a book?

2. Explain how God's authority was transferred between one Guru and the next.

Summary

You should now know about different sources of authority in Sikhism and have thought about their importance.

6.10 Evaluation of leadership

Objectives

Summarise and evaluate different forms of authority and leadership.

A *Founders of religions have had special experiences*

Throughout this chapter, you have looked at different types of leadership and analysed the source of the authority the leaders have. In the theistic religions, God is the ultimate source of authority, inspiring those who lead through their work or in writing the content of holy books. In Buddhism, which is atheistic, the authority is believed to come from within rather than externally.

Founders

Apart from Hinduism, each religion has a founder who underwent experiences that no ordinary person undergoes. They may have been an ordinary person to start with, but they certainly were changed by their experiences. In Christianity, it is believed that their founder Jesus is God himself; so if that is true, his authority is clear. The others – Siddattha Gotama, Muhammad, Moses (and Abraham) and Guru Nanak – all had deeply spiritual experiences; Siddattha Gotama through meditation, the others through God's intervention in their lives. All developed a great desire to tell others of their experiences and offered a new way of life based upon the inspiration and authority they had gained from them. Nobody knows how Hinduism, the most ancient of the six religions, started, or even whether it actually had a founder.

Holy books

Of the millions of books that have ever been written, few have the special status of being holy books. Writers have written books of experiences, teachings or interpretations of teachings that fall short of being a holy book, whereas other books have achieved that status. Four Gospels were chosen to be in the Christian Bible, but many more were rejected, and many poets wrote hymns and poems that were not included in the Bible, the Guru Granth Sahib or the Smriti scriptures. The writings that were chosen were immediately given special status and authority by being considered to be holy.

AQA Examiner's tip

Although this page is about all six religions, you are advised to use just two religions in any question. The two religions you choose can vary from question to question.

Research activity

Using the internet or a library, find out more about the special experience that the founders of two religions you are studying went through.

Chapter 6   Religious authority   137

B Some leaders believe they have a calling from God

Authority
Leadership
Ordained
Shruti
Smriti
Sunnah
Shari'ah
Talmud
Bet Din
Guru
Dalai Lama
Pope
Qur'an
Guru Granth Sahib
Sangha
Bible
Imam
Pandit
Rabbi

Human leaders today

Every religion has leaders today. Most of them work within the community, attached to a place of worship. Followers expect their leaders to have authority to undertake the tasks they perform. In all cases, some of their authority comes from their in-depth learning about their faith and the way of life and morality it encourages, but in some cases it is more than that. Some leaders believe they have a calling from God to perform this role. Christian priests are given special powers when they become priests, Buddhist monks choose a different style of living from lay Buddhists, and are thought by Theravada Buddhists to be closer to enlightenment. Whatever the reason, these people are accepted in their special position and respected by believers. Many people trust their wellbeing to them and use their advice and teachings in their quest for spiritual truth or closeness to God.

Activities

1. a Which do you think has the most authority?
   - Founders of the faith
   - Holy books
   - Human leaders today

   Explain your opinion.

   b Which of these do you think is the easiest to take advice from? Give reasons for your answer.

2. 'Religious leaders today do not have any special authority – they are just like anybody else.' Do you agree? Give reasons for your answer, showing you have thought about more than one point of view.

Summary

You should now be able to think about and evaluate three types of religious leadership and the authority that believers think they have.

Activity

3. If there are any words here that you don't know, try to find them in this chapter.

Assessment guidance

6

Religious authority – summary

With reference to at least **two** of the religions you have studied, for the examination you should now be able to:

✔ understand and explain religious ideas about the value and need for leadership and authority in religion

✔ explain the role and importance of different sources of religious leadership and authority, including:
- human sources
- historical sources, including founders
- tradition and community
- holy books

✔ consider how these sources of authority impact in the modern world

✔ evaluate the relative worth and effectiveness of these different sources of leadership and authority.

Sample answer

1 Write an answer to the following examination question:

'No source of religious leadership has authority.'

Do you agree? Give reasons for your answer, showing that you have thought about more than one point of view. Refer to religious arguments in your answer.

(6 marks)

2 Read the following sample answer:

> I find it hard to agree with the statement. Of course religious leaders, especially founders of religions have authority. Christians believe that Jesus was God, so how much more authority can you expect? Something happened to the Buddha when he said he was enlightened – you don't change like that for nothing.
>
> However, all we know about these people is from the holy books that tell us about their lives. Of course these could be wrong and we could all have been conned for centuries.
>
> In conclusion, I think that some religious leaders have authority but maybe not all of them.

3 With a partner, discuss the sample answer. Do you think that there are other things that the student could have included in the answer?

4 What mark would you give this answer out of 6? (Look at the mark scheme in the Introduction on page 7 (AO2) before you attempt this.) What are the reasons for the mark you have given?

AQA Examination-style questions

1 Look at the photograph and answer the following questions.

    (a) Name **two** religions and **one** holy book from each. *(2 marks)*

    (b) Explain why a holy book is important as a source of authority for believers. *(4 marks)*

> **AQA Examiner's tip:** When you are asked to explain, you need to give details and possibly examples to support your point. You will need to include at least two detailed points.

    (c) 'A human leader is better than a book.' What do you think? Explain your opinion. *(3 marks)*

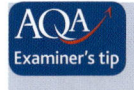

> **AQA Examiner's tip:** Remember that when you are asked for your opinion, you will only get marks for the reasons you give. Try to write one well-developed reason or several simple ones, or a mixture of both. Note that this question does not ask for more than one point of view.

    (d) Explain the role of a present-day human religious leader. *(3 marks)*

> **AQA Examiner's tip:** You need to include detail to support either two points or one very well-developed point. You could give an example if you think this might help.

    (e) 'The founders of religion should be respected because they had God's authority.'

        Do you agree? Give reasons for your answer, showing that you have thought about more than one point of view. Refer to religious arguments in your answer. *(6 marks)*

> **AQA Examiner's tip:** You need to think carefully of reasons why some people believe that having God's authority means founders of religion should be respected and reasons why others may disagree. You may also think about whether they did have God's authority or not.

Glossary

A

Adhan: the Muslim call to prayer, five times a day.

Adi Granth: the first collection of Sikh scriptures.

Adonai: Lord: in Judaism, the name used to address God in prayer.

Adoration: worship, a feeling of profound love and admiration (for God).

Allah: the Islamic name for God.

Apostles' Creed: a statement setting out the beliefs of the Christian faith, based on the central teachings of the apostles.

Ark (aron hakodesh): where the Torah scrolls are kept in the synagogue (Judaism).

Arti (arati): a welcoming ceremony in which items such as lamps or incense are offered to the deity or saintly people (Hinduism).

Atman: self. Can refer to the body, mind or soul depending on context. Usually the inner, or real, self (Hinduism).

Aum (Om): sacred symbol and sound, which represents the Ultimate (Hinduism).

Authority: the power exercised by someone who advises or has leadership over others.

B

Bhikkhu (bhikshu): a fully ordained Buddhist monk.

Bhikkhuni (bhishuni): a fully ordained Buddhist nun.

Bible: sacred book of Christians containing both the Old and New Testaments.

Bimah: a desk or platform for the reading of the Torah (Judaism).

Brahman: the ultimate reality from which everything comes and into which everything will return (Hinduism).

Buddha: historically the Buddha – the enlightened one; an awakened or enlightened person.

C

Catacombs: underground burial chambers for early Christians and Jews.

Cathedral: the principal/main church of a bishop's diocese.

Celibacy: not having sex; the decision to remain unmarried or refrain from having sex for religious reasons.

Ceremony: a ritualistic service.

Chapel: a place of Christian worship, sometimes inside a church; a plain building used instead of a Church in some Protestant traditions.

Church: the Holy People of God, also called the Body of Christ, among whom Christ is present and active; members of a particular Christian denomination/tradition; a building in which Christians worship.

Cleanliness: keeping free from impurities and anything that is dishonourable.

Community: a group within which a person lives and acts, e.g. a religious community.

Compassion: loving kindness. A feeling of sympathy that makes one want to help.

Confession: admitting to God (via a priest in a Roman Catholic Church) one's sins and faults. Term used for a type of prayer (Christianity).

Corporate worship: worship performed together as a congregation.

Covenant: a binding agreement made in the presence of God; God's agreement to look after the Jews as his chosen people and, in return, the Jews' agreement to obey God (Judaism).

Cross: a symbol of the sacrifice of Jesus at his crucifixion; the object on which Jesus was crucified (Christianity).

D

Deities: gods or images of gods (Hinduism).

Denomination: a group of religious congregations having its own organisation and a distinctive Christian faith.

Devotee: a person showing devotion, a believer.

Devotion: religious worship.

Du'a: personal prayer (Islam).

E

Eightfold Path: the way to wisdom; mental training and the way of morality (eight stages to be practised simultaneously) (Buddhism).

F

Five Ks: five symbols worn by Sikhs: uncut hair (kesh), steel bangle (kara), wooden comb (kangha), sword (kirpan) and white shorts (kachera).

Five Moral Precepts: in Buddhism, these are to not kill any living being, refrain from stealing, refrain from wrongful sexual activity, refrain from lying, and not taking drugs and alcohol that cloud the mind.

Five Pillars of Islam: the five most important duties: to believe, to pray, to give to charity, to fast and to go on pilgrimage (Islam).

Five Takhts: five gurdwaras or 'royal thrones' considered to be the seat of Sikh authority where decisions are made.

Font: the receptacle holding water used for baptism (Christianity).

Four Aims of Life: in Hinduism, the aims of life are religious duty (dharma), creating wealth (artha), enjoyment (kama), and achieving moksha.

Four Ashrams: in Hinduism, the four stages of life: student (brahmachari), householder (grihasta), forest dweller (vanaprashta) and someone who gives up everything (sannyasa).

Glossary

Four Noble Truths: dukkha, tanha, nirodha, magga (suffering, the cause of suffering, the end of suffering, the path to the end of suffering) (Buddhism).

Four Varnas: the four main divisions of Hindu society: Brahmins (priests), Kshatriyas (rulers and warriors), Vaishyas (merchants and farmers) and Shudras (labourers).

G

Goal of life: the aim or purpose of someone's life.

Gurdwara: the Sikh place of worship. Literally 'the doorway to the Guru'.

Guru: a Sikh religious teacher.

Guru Granth Sahib: collection of Sikh scriptures, collated by Guru Arjan and Guru Gobind Singh.

H

Hadith: sayings of the Prophet Muhammad. A major source of Islamic Law.

Hajj: the annual pilgrimage to Makkah, one of the five pillars of Islam.

Halal: meat that is prepared in the correct way for Muslims to eat.

HaShem: in Judaism, the word for God used in ordinary conversation. It means 'The Name'.

Heaven: eternal life with God (Christianity).

Hell: eternal separation from God (Christianity).

Holy Communion: a service of thanksgiving in which the sacrificial death and resurrection of Jesus is celebrated using bread and wine (Christianity).

Honesty: being truthful and just, not cheating or stealing.

I

Imam: a person who leads communal prayer.

Initiation: being entered formally into a religion.

J

Judgement Day: the time when God will decide whether people go to heaven or hell.

Jumu'ah: weekly communal salah performed after midday on a Friday (Islam).

Justice: bringing about what is right, fair, according to the law or making up for what has been done wrong.

K

Kama: having a regulated sense of enjoyment and pleasure, including erotic love, in order to be healthy and fulfilled – the third aim of life (Hinduism).

Kamma (karma): literally 'action'; deliberate actions that affect the believer's circumstances in this and future lives; cause and effect (Buddhism).

Karma: action. The law of cause and effect (Hinduism); that a person reaps what they sow (Sikhism).

Khalsa: the Sikh community, founded by Guru Gobind Singh in 1699 C.E. Literally 'the community of the pure'.

Kosher: food that conforms to Jewish dietary laws.

L

Langar: the dining hall of the gurdwara and the food served there. Literally 'Guru's kitchen' (Sikhism).

Leadership: taking the role of directing others in tasks or activities.

M

Madrassah: school or college for Islamic education.

Mala beads: string of beads used as a prayer aid (Buddhism, Hinduism and Sikhism).

Mandir: a Hindu temple.

Mantra: a short prayer/chant repeated as an aid to meditation, such as Om Mani Padme Hum in Buddhism.

Martyr: to put someone to death for their beliefs; someone who is martyred.

Maschiach (Messiah): in Judaism, God's chosen king (anointed one) who will bring about a new age of peace in the world.

Meditation: a special form of concentration or prayer which uses very few or no words.

Menorah: candle-holder with seven branches. It is often placed prominently in the synagogue as a reminder of the Jewish Temple.

Merit-making: the process of deserving, earned by service or performance.

Mitzvot: in Judaism, the commandments that are in God's Law (the Torah). There are 613 in total.

Monotheism: belief in one God.

Mosque: the Muslim place of worship.

Muhammad: the last and greatest of the prophets of Allah; Muhammad means 'praised' (Islam).

Murti (Moorti): image or deity used as a focus of worship and offerings (Hinduism).

Mysticism: using prayer and meditation to achieve such a close relationship with God that the person is not aware of him/herself any more.

N

Nibbana (nirvana): the state of perfect peace which results from ending all greed, hatred and ignorance (Buddhism).

Nit nem: daily specified prayers (Sikhism).

O

Omnibenevolent: the characteristic of God that he loves everyone (all-loving).

Omnipotence: the characteristic of God that he is all-powerful.

Omniscient: the characteristic of God that he knows everything (all-knowing).

P

Pandit: a learned Hindu, in philosophy, religion and history.

Pilgrimage: a journey made for religious reasons.

Place of worship: a building or other location where an individual or a group of people comes to perform acts of religious worship.

Glossary

Prayer: words of praise, thanks or sorrow etc. offered to God or to the gods.

Priest: the person who leads the service in Catholic, Orthodox and Church of England services (Christianity).

Prostrate: lie on the ground face down to show reverence and humility.

Puja: Hindu worship in the home or temple.

Purgatory: a place where souls go to be purified from their sins before they go to heaven (Christianity).

Q

Qur'an: the Holy Book revealed to the Prophet Muhammad by the angel Jibril. Allah's final revelation to humankind (Islam).

R

Rabbi: a Jewish religious leader and teacher.

Relic: an object of religious veneration, especially a piece of the body or a personal item of a holy person.

Religious leaders: the people who lead the various faiths.

Respect: showing consideration for others' feelings, views or beliefs.

Resurrection of the body: the belief that God will raise everyone to life before the Judgement. Life after this will be in a perfect body that does not die.

Rites of passage: ceremonies associated with the major moments in life such as birth, marriage and death.

Ritual bathing: bathing according to a certain set pattern or religious rule.

S

Sacred texts: writings which are believed to originate from God or a god.

Salah: prayer to and worship of Allah, performed under the conditions set by the Prophet Muhammad. The second pillar of Islam.

Samsara: the circle of birth, death and re-birth, which can be transcended by following the Eightfold Path (Buddhism).

Sangat: congregation in a gurdwara (Sikhism).

Sefer Torah: torah scroll kept in the ark (Judaism).

Shrine: a place of worship considered holy because of its link with some sacred person or thing.

Soul: the spiritual part of a person that continues after death.

Spiritual: concerned with the mind or spirit, and/or religious matters, rather than the physical body; the opposite of material.

Stupa: a burial mound (Buddhism).

symbolism: when an image or action stands for something else.

synagogue: building for Jewish public prayer, study and gathering.

T

Takht: the throne where the Guru Granth Sahib is placed when it is open. The Five Takhts are places of authority in Sikhism. The Akal Takht (Throne of the Eternal) in Amritsar is the main one.

Talmud: the written version of the oral instructions (Mishnah) passed down from Moses along with the commentary on them (Gemara) (Judaism).

Tawhid: in Islam, the belief that God is One, without parts or divisions.

Tefillin: small leather boxes containing extracts from the Torah, strapped to the believer's arm and forehead for morning prayers (Judaism).

Ten Commandments: a list of ten rules believed to have been given by God to Moses on Mount Sinai (Christianity and Judaism).

The Three Marks of Existence: the truth about all things. They do not last (anicca), they have no soul that lives on after death (anatta) and they result in suffering (dukkha) (Buddhism).

Three Refuges: Buddhist bhikkhus and bhikkhunis 'take refuge' in three things: the Buddha, the Dhamma and the Sangha (the Three Jewels).

Tithing: giving a tenth of one's income to charity or to support the religion.

Tolerance: willingness to permit other views, beliefs and opinions.

Torah: the five books of Moses and first section of the Tenakh – the law; the whole of Jewish teaching.

Trimurti: three Hindu gods (Brahma, Vishnu and Shiva) who control three main aspects of existence – creation, preservation and destruction.

Tripitaka: Buddhist scriptures divided into three collections.

U

Ummah: all Muslims are regarded as part of a brotherhood; the nation of Islam.

V

Vegan: a person who will not use any animal product.

Vegetarian: a person that does not eat meat.

Vipassana (vipashyana): reaching an insight into the true nature of things through meditation (Buddhism).

Vows: a solemn promise.

W

Western Wall: the only remaining part of the second Temple in Jerusalem (Judaism).

Wisdom: showing soundness of judgement.

Worship: acts of religious praise, honour or devotion.

Y

Yad: a pointer used when reading the Torah scrolls (Judaism).

Z

Zion: a term referring to the land of Israel and Jerusalem, including the Temple (Judaism).

Index

A
Abraham 76, 77
afterlife 92–93
akhirah 93
Allah 77, 79, 130
altars 15
Amritsar, India 68–69
Apostles' Creed 82–83
Aqiqah ceremony 107
ashrams 107, 108
atman 92
authority 118–119, 136, 212
   different religions 124–135

B
Baisakhi (Vaisakhi) 115
baptism 15, 106
Bar Mitzvah 65, 107
Bat Mitzvah 26, 107
beliefs 78–93
Benares, India 55, 60
Bet Din 133
Bethlehem 56
bhikkhuni 38–39, 97
bhikkhus 38–39, 97, 124
Bible 127
birth ceremonies 106–107
Bismillah 107
Bodh Gaya, India 55
bodhisattvas 38, 78, 96
Brahman 16, 60–61, 78
Buddha 54–55, 74–75, 78
Buddhism
   authority 124–125
   beliefs 78, 80–81, 92
   holy places 54–55
   origins 74, 74–75
   places of worship 12–13
   practices 96, 102, 110
   prayer 36, 36–37, 104
   rites of passage 106, 108
   worship 30, 32, 34, 38–39

C
caste system 85, 128
Christianity
   authority 121, 126–127
   beliefs 78, 82–83, 92
   holy places 56–59
   origins 74, 77
   places of worship 14–15
   practices 97, 102, 110–111
   prayer 35, 36, 104
   rites of passage 106, 108
   worship 30–31, 32, 34, 40–41
Christmas 110–111
Church of England 127
circumcision 107
codes and duties 96–101

D
Dalai Lama 70, 120, 124
dharma 84, 85
dietary laws 102–103
Diwali 34, 112, 114

E
Easter 111
Eid ul Adha 113
Eid ul Fitr 112–113
Eightfold Path 80, 81

F
festivals 110–115
Five Ks 90–91
Five Moral Precepts 97
Five Pillars 44, 86–87, 99
Five Takhts 23, 67
Four Noble Truths 80
four varnas 84–85
funerals 108, 109

G
Ganges river 60
Golden Temple 9, 22, 68–69
gurdwaras 22–23, 27, 48–49, 67
Guru Granth Sahib 23, 48–49, 79, 107, 123, 134, 135
Guru Nanak 68, 75, 134
Gurus 134
Gutka 48

H
Hadith 44, 98, 131
Hajj 62, 69, 87, 99
halal meat 102–103
havan 42, 43
Hinduism
   authority 128–129
   beliefs 78, 84–85, 92
   holy places 60–61
   origins 74
   places of worship 10, 16–17, 43
   practices 98, 102, 112
   prayer 36, 104–105
   rites of passage 107, 108
   worship 30, 32, 34, 42–43
Holi 112
Holocaust 89
holy books 122, 123, 136
   different religions 122–123, 125, 127, 129, 131, 132–133, 135
Holy Communion 40, 41

I
icons 14, 34
imams 44, 130
initiation 106–107
Islam
   authority 122–123, 130–131
   beliefs 79, 86–87, 93
   holy places 62–63
   origins 74, 77
   places of worship 18–19
   practices 98–99, 102–103, 112–113
   prayer 36, 105
   rites of passage 107, 109
   worship 31, 32, 44–45

J
Japji 79
Jerusalem 57, 63, 64–65
Jesus Christ 56, 57, 77, 82–83
Judaism
   authority 132–133
   beliefs 79, 88–89, 93
   holy places 64–65
   origins 74, 76
   places of worship 20–21
   practices 100, 103, 114
   prayer 35, 37, 105

Index

rites of passage 107, 109
worship 31, 33, 34, 46–47
Judgement Day 92, 93

K
Ka'aba 19, 62
karma 92
Khalsa 90
kosher food 103
Krishna 61
Kumbh Mela festival 60
Kurahit 91, 101, 103
Kushinagara, India 55

L
langar 27, 49
leadership 118, 119
  evaluation of 136–137
  holy books and 122–123
  of religions 120–135
life after death 92–93
Lourdes, France 59
Lumbini, Nepal 54

M
Madinah, Saudi Arabia 62
Makkah, Saudi Arabia 62
mandalas 34
mandirs 10, 16, 17, 43, 128
mantras 36, 36–37
marriages 108, 109
Mathura, India 61
meditation 35, 38, 104–105
mitzvot 100, 132
Moses 76, 77
mosques 18–19, 44–45, 63, 130
Muhammad 76, 77, 131
murtis 16, 17, 42, 120
Muslims see Islam

N
nibbana (nirvana) 75, 92, 96
nisham sahib 22
nit nem 105

O
Om (Aum) 16, 42

P
pandits 128
Pesach (Passover) 114

pilgrimage 52–53
  holy places 54–67
  impact and value of 68–71
places of worship 8–9
  in the community 26–27
  different religions 12–23
  money spent on 10–11
  value of 24–25
Prayag, India 60–61
prayer 35, 36–37, 104–105
puja 16, 38, 42, 128
purgatory 92

Q
Qur'an 44, 98, 122–123, 131

R
rabbis 46, 133
rak'ahs 45
Ramadan 27, 86, 112
rangolis 34
resurrection 92, 109
rites of passage 26, 106–109
ritual bathing 60–61
Roman Catholics 58, 120, 126
Rome, Italy 58
Rosary beads 36
Rosh Hashanah 114

S
salah 44, 86, 99
samatha 38
sangha 39, 124
sawm 86, 99
Shabbat (Sabbath) 33, 46
Shahadah 86, 99
Shari'ah 98, 131
Shema 37, 88
Sheol 93
shrines 8, 12, 16
Shruti scriptures 129
Sikhism
  authority 133, 134–135
  beliefs 79, 90–91, 92
  holy places 68–69
  origins 74, 75
  places of worship 22–23
  practices 101, 103, 114–115
  prayer 36, 105
  rites of passage 107, 109
  worship 30, 33, 48–49

singing bowls 34
Sirat Bridge 93
Smriti scriptures 129
Songkran 110
soul 92–93
stupas 12–13
Sunnah 131
synagogues 20–21, 46

T
Talmud 133
teaching, religious 26
tefillin 37
temples 12
  Buddhist 12–13
  Hindu 10, 16, 17, 43
Ten Commandments 21, 97
Three Marks of Existence 80
Three Refugees 96
tithing 96, 97, 101
Torah 20, 46–47, 76, 88, 100, 132
Trimurti 78
Trinity 78
Tripitaka 125
tzedek 100

U
ummah 44, 77, 87, 112

V
Varanasi, India 55, 60
vipassana (vipashyana) 38

W
Wesak (Vesak) 110
Western Wall, Jerusalem 64–65
worship 30–31
  aids to 34–37
  days of 32–33
  different religions 38–49
wudu (wuzu) 45

Y
yad 34
Yad Vashem, Jerusalem 65
yoga 104–105
Yom Kippur 114

Z
zakah 86, 99